THE GIFTH

CW00432776

WOMEN'S STUDIES BOOKS OF RELATED INTEREST

Bureaucrats, technocrats, femocrats
Anna Yeatman

Dissenting opinions
Régina Graycar

Educating girls: Practice and research
Edited by Gilah C Leder and Shirley N Sampson

Female crime: The construction of women in criminology
Nagire Naffine

Feminine/masculine and representation
Edited by Terry Threadgold and Anne Cranny-Francis

For and against feminism: A personal journey into feminist theory and history
Ann Curthoys

Frogs and snails and feminist tales
Bronwyn Davies

Gender and power: Society, the person and sexual politics
R W Connell

Law and the sexes: Explorations in feminist jurisprudence
Ngaire Naffine

Playing the state: Australian feminist interventions
Edited by Sophie Watson

Populate and perish: Australian women's fight for birth control
Stefania Siedlecky and Diana Wyndham

Same difference: Feminism and sexual difference
Carol Bacchi

Secretaries talk: Sexuality, power and work
Rosemary Pringle

Sexual subversions: Three French feminists
Elizabeth Grosz

Short-changed: Women and economic policies
Rhonda Sharp and Ray Broomhill

Sisters in suits: Women and public policy in Australia
Marian Sawer

Staking a claim: Feminism, bureaucracy and the state
Suzanne Franzway, Dianne Court and R W Connell

THE GIFTHORSE

A critical look at Equal Employment Opportunity in Australia

Gretchen Poiner and Sue Wills

ALLEN & UNWIN

© Gretchen Poiner and Sue Wills, 1991
This book is copyright under the Berne Convention.
No reproduction without permission. All rights reserved.

First published 1991
Allen & Unwin Australia Pty Ltd
8 Napier Street, North Sydney NSW 2059 Australia

National Library of Australia
Cataloguing-in-Publication entry:

Poiner, Gretchen.
    The gifthorse: a critical look at equal employment opportunity in Australia.

    Bibliography.
    Includes index.
    ISBN 0 04 442298 8.

    1. Discrimination in employment — Australia.
    2. Affirmative action programs — Australia.
    3. Women — Employment — Australia. 4. Sex discrimination in
    employment — Australia. I. Wills, Sue. II. Title.

331·1330994

Library of Congress Catalog Card No: 90−062231

Set in 10/11pt Baskerville by Setrite Typesetters, Hong Kong
Printed by SRM Production Services Sdn Bhd, Malaysia

Contents

Acknowledgments

This work has been a cooperative enterprise. With two authors this is a statement of the obvious but collaboration has extended beyond our mutual effort to include many others who have contributed directly and indirectly to the endeavour. We have certainly been much encouraged by our numerous friends and colleagues who felt the time had come to have a closer look at EEO and the expectations and criticisms which had grown up around it. This list is very long and to present it runs the danger of exclusion. We therefore thank, on a collective basis, but no less warmly for that, all those who gave us such sustained and sustaining support.

There are others whose contribution deserves acknowledgment but who remain nameless because they specifically requested anonymity. This they did because of their employment, whether in the public or in the private sector, a contract they believed might be jeopardised by their outspokenness. We value greatly their information and their insights.

Some names can be spoken and we are indebted to Nerida Blair, Victoria Gollan, Joanna Kalowski and Nada Spasojevic for their perceptive comments on disadvantaging processes, and to Heather Greenfield, Sharon Sullivan and Barbara Wertheim for their informed perceptions. Among those organisations whose cooperation was appreciated we thank CSR, ESSO, IBM and Qantas.

We are certainly grateful for the professional skills of Vivien Robinson and Di Salisbury who were, mercifully, able to transform our drafts into readable manuscript.

The order of the authors' names was determined by the toss of a coin. If each of us had to single out one person whose hard work, patience, good humour, support and friendship had been crucial to the completion of this endeavour, each of us would have no hesitation in naming the other.

Beforeword or betimes

Being an explanation of why we have done this thing.

Why are we doing this thing?

In this work we turn a critical eye to Equal Employment Opportunity (EEO) legislation and practice. The question to be answered is why do so? The reason quite simply is that EEO needs to be subjected to reasoned critical appraisal and put into perspective. A gifthorse from governments to various disadvantaged groups, it should be looked squarely in the mouth.

We distinguish between equal employment opportunity and Equal Employment Opportunity in terms of the latter being formal legislative attempts to achieve the former. In Australia, unlike the United States of America, EEO was born of the political action of feminists. Whatever its claims, women have been its primary focus and the brief history of EEO in this country is principally about women's participation in employment. Our work inevitably reflects this bias. Outside the availability of information it is not our intention to give primacy to any group. Indeed we see the conflation of various groups into one category as improper on several grounds, one of which is that it does not serve equally the interests of all groups. There are, of course, means in addition to EEO laws and the programs they establish which have been, and are being, pursued in an attempt to achieve equal opportunity in employment. But partly because of the media attention EEO has attracted these are less well developed and harder to place on the political agenda. This is doubly regrettable. Some of them, like widely available childcare and changes to the division of domestic labour, are prerequisites (or at the very least corequisites) to EEO programs. Secondly, so much public emphasis on EEO narrows to a squint the much broader feminist visions out of which it arose. EEO is not really what the Women's Liberation Movement was all about, nor do most feminists see it as 'the solution': equal opportunity in employment is itself a prerequisite, something which it is desirable to have while those broader visions of a just society are being worked out. In and of itself, EEO for example will do little to reduce the Aboriginal infant mortality rate, will do little to end racism and ethnic prejudice, will do little to end male violence against women or to reduce the disabling effects of so many workplace practices.

Until now, reactions to EEO have fallen into three main groups. All attach far greater importance to it than it warrants. The first reaction is one of unrelenting hostility and opposition. The second reflects the kind of cargo cult mentality which sees EEO as 'the solution' or at least as bringing 'the solution' inexorably in its train. And the third reaction is to treat EEO as a sacred cow. The first two reactions entail a good deal of misunderstanding about what EEO can and cannot achieve. The third may be aware of the limits to what EEO can achieve and indeed, to what it has achieved, but it is a reaction which rarely participates in the public debate lest its reservations be taken up by those hostile to EEO and used to reverse all of the steps made toward creating a less unjust society. We think it is time to look more closely at the sacred cow.

Unrelenting hostility

Those who were implacably opposed to the enactment of EEO laws in Australia drew quite heavily for their fears on what they believed happened as a consequence of the introduction of Affirmative Action in the United States of America some twenty years ago. The bogeyman of quotas in employment is perhaps less frightening than the dread of undermining the traditional nuclear family and threatening democracy. All have been seen as consequences of EEO or Affirmative Action in the USA.

Letters published in the pages of *Quadrant* from correspondents in a range of US cities tell of some of the excesses and genuinely ludicrous situations which have arisen there. All they illustrate is that Affirmative Action in the United States is well integrated into a culture which produces all kinds of excesses. But many assert more:

> Australia should learn the lessons first, that for practical purposes (which are all that matter here!) there is no such thing as affirmative action which falls short of positive discrimination; second, there is no question but that the merit principle is a casualty; and third, the biggest political obstacle that faces those who, even with popular mandate, wish to dismantle it, is the tenacity of the clerks charged with implementing it. (Slater 1986:44−45)

Even more colourful are the diatribes against EEO (among other things) to be found in the *Endeavour Forum Newsletter* put out by Women Who Want to be Women. Under the headline 'Affirmative Action Hoax Exposed' Babette Francis railed (incorrectly) that affirmative action means that equal opportunity officers can order that women be given preference in employment and promotion, even

over better qualified men, until men and women are equally represented in all jobs and at every level of promotion (40; May 1987:3).
Very few people read *Quadrant* or the *Endeavour Forum Newsletter* and by
and large the mass media do not pick up material from them. The
most likely place to find slightly reworked versions of their prophecies
is in the pages of Hansard, a tribute to the lobbying skills of Women
Who Want to Be Women and the men who want women to want to
be women. Then again, very few people read Hansard or listen to
parliamentary debates.

Cargo cultists

The flip side to the prophecies of the end of Western civilisation which
opponents saw as the inevitable consequence of EEO are the extravagant hopes of some of its proponents. Indeed, some of the rhetoric
the Commonwealth Labor Government employed to sell its Affirmative
Action legislation comes perilously close to promising gains the legislation simply cannot deliver. Increased economic effectiveness, reduced
turnover and absenteeism, increased productivity and profitability for
employers; greater freedom of choice, new career structures and increased job satisfaction for employees; and expanded membership for
unions are all cited (Department of Prime Minister and Cabinet, Vol.
I 1984:16−17). And the benefits do not stop at employment—they
are said to flow on to the rest of the community. As Ann Game
summarised the rhetoric which only just fell short of promising an
affirmative action-led economic recovery: 'Women's skills have been
underutilised and this is a waste of resources. What is good for
women is good for the "economy", "our progress", and "good management"' (Game, 1984:254).

But it is only rhetoric. The government had to convince women
(the group covered) that it was doing something on their behalf which
would mean real change. At the same time it had to convince the
private sector that the legislation did not really mean such change for
them and certainly not the kind of change they would reject if they
really thought about the benefits it would bring them.

Women's groups involved in lobbying for legislation spent much of
their time not questioning what the legislation might or might not
achieve but urging the incorporation of stronger penalties. In other
words, there seemed to be little doubt that if it was adhered to the
legislation would bring real and substantial benefits to all women.
What was in doubt, so far as affirmative action was concerned, was
not the benefits but whether employers covered by the legislation
would comply with its requirements when the only penalty for not

doing so was to be named in Parliament. Basically the attitude is one of cargo cultists. Arrestingly, a critical feature of cargo cults is their conservatism, overriding their radical potential (Lawrence, 1964: 224–251). Wealth and power will be redistributed, but there is no intention of replacing the old order of exchange with a fundamentally different structure. It is really a question of equalising benefits while preserving basic principles and systems.

Both of these first two reactions to EEO are in large measure reactions to Affirmative Action in the United States, the first a reaction of fear, the second one of hope. Both seem to be based on a reading of a very limited range of material—spectacular legal decisions and bizarre antics picked up by the mass media. At best, systematic studies of the results of Affirmative Action Programs in the United States are contradictory or inconclusive; at worst, they seem to indicate little change at all and even less that can be directly attributable to those programs.

> Male doctors, lawyers, financial managers and college teachers all make between 22% and 35% more than females in the same occupations. Service, sales and administrative support are predominantly women's work, but even there men make more than women. In 1985 the median income for women who completed 4 years of college was less than that for men who completed high school. That's been true since 1970 according to Census figures compiled by the AFL-CIO. For the same number of years of schooling completed, the difference in income between men and women in 1985 was about $9,000. For college graduates the difference was $11,433. (*Off Our Backs*, July 1988:4)

EEO as sacred cow

The most we can say about the effectiveness of Affirmative Action Programs in the United States is that they may have contributed to improving the lot of some members of some of the groups covered by them, as far as employment is concerned. We can also say that the programs are fairly costly in terms of money and in terms of the toll they take on their alleged beneficiaries; that they are subject to manipulation as the flavour of US administrations change; that they only work, or work best, in economic good times; and that a lingering death will result from inadequate resources allocated to their implementation.

That being the rosiest picture that can be painted of the US experience, this is no time to treat EEO/AA in Australia as a sacred cow. There are similarities between the pieces of legislation enacted in Australia and the US, more so in New South Wales than at the

Commonwealth level. For example, both in New South Wales and in the US a ragbag has been made of several social categories labelled 'disadvantaged'. There is no argument against the fact that race, ethnic background, sex and physical disability are often enough made the grounds for discrimination. By no means, however, are the problems confronting members of these groups the same. To apply the same corrective measures to diverse social groups enduring various forms of social disadvantage borne of quite different experiences is not likely to be equally effective for each of the groups. In medicine broad spectrum antibiotics are prescribed when the medical practitioner is not quite sure which nasties are causing the problem. We have a clear enough idea of the different causes of disadvantage for the different groups lumped together in the legislation to warrant separate remedies for separate conditions of disadvantage. There is little point insisting on numerical employment targets for Aboriginal academics when a bigger problem facing Aborigines is surviving infancy and in that happy event, acquiring even elementary education.

Even if we put to one side the confused picture we have of the US experience we need to ask ourselves whether EEO can achieve eeo and if so, in what form and at what cost? Further, what would eeo mean? Is it possible to have equal employment opportunity within a fundamentally unchanged and basically unjust society? The people in New South Wales who have been associated with that state's version of EEO have for the most part been publicly silent about its shortcomings. Many of them were keen for a book of this nature to be written — by people other than themselves. Most are employed in one area or the other of the New South Wales public service concerned with the administration of social policy; some are in private sector organisations. All spoke freely with us on one condition — that they not be thanked by name for their help.

1

Back to basics

Being a discussion of the basic concepts of equality and inequality, equity, equal opportunity in employment, discrimination and affirmative action, and a discussion of some dirty words — target, quota, prefential treatment and reverse discimination.

Equality and inequality

The theme of equality — or more precisely inequality — has over time run as a warp thread through the reflections and analyses of social philosophers and sociologists. At a simple conceptual level two forms of human inequality are commonly identified — social inequality and natural differences. The distinction between them is drawn on the basis of the causes or origins of the form of inequality. In the case of social inequality the causes are seen to lie in social, hence mutable, arrangements.

Social inequality, as Béteille points out, has both a distributive and a relational aspect. The first aspect is concerned with how factors such as income, wealth, occupation, education, power, skills and the like are socially distributed. The relational aspect refers to how these criteria affect social interaction (1969:13). Needless to say, the relational dimension of social inequality in turn defines more sharply the distributive profile as groups of privileged people seek to secure their advantage.

In the case of human inequality born of natural difference, the causes are much more contested. Indeed, the simple conceptual distinction between the two forms of human inequality breaks down under the weight of claim and counterclaim about just how many natural differences are really disguised forms of social inequality or minor natural differences amplified and distorted by social arrangements. At stake are beliefs about the desirability, even the possibility, of different sets of social arrangements. As Dahrendorf points out, an ideology of social inequality, premised on natural difference is to this day, and in one form or another,

invoked by all societies that are worried about their survival to

reassure themselves of the justice of their injustices. By repeating
'in a simplified form the errors of Aristotle, such societies assert a
pre-established harmony of things natural and social, and above
all a congruence of natural differences between men and social
differences between their positions. (1969:18)

While Dahrendorfs interest in inequality relates essentially to
stratification and certainly does not encompass the inequality of
women, Aborigines, migrants or people with disabilities, his argument
applies at a general level which includes sex and ethnicity as well as
class considerations. But the view he criticises is not simply a passive
form of self-vindication; as ideology it actively serves the interests of
dominant groups. Justification of inequality by reference to the
naturalness of its bases eliminates any need for sociological explanation
and no doubt serves as something of a gobstopper in philosophical
enquiry. The question of corrective social action is, of course, made
irrelevant. If all the differences between the sexes, for example, are
immutable in the sense that they are genetically determined, then no
amount of effort expended in attempting to rearrange the social order
to provide expanded opportunities for women will, in the long term,
be successful. Worse, argue some opponents of such changes, the very
attempt will be destructive of the social order of men but especially of
women, who will be forced to try to perform feats of which they are
as genetically incapable as a fish is of riding a bicycle.

There is another ideological facet to the issue of social/natural
inequality. Intriguingly in this case, systems of unequal social rights
and rewards lead to an emphasis on egalitarianism, in some circumstances on the part of underprivileged people, in others by dominant
groups. In a cross-cultural analysis, Jayawardena (1968) examined
the relationship of equality of social condition and the doctrine of
equal human worth. Among the communities he studied he found
that, in circumstances of marked social difference and inequality, the
dominated groups stressed a common and intrinsic human worth. He
saw it as providing the basis for group action and the moral source
of norms guiding interpersonal relationships. But it also happens that
dominant groups may see it as in their interest to promote the idea of
natural equality. In Australian rural society, for example, the employer
is quite likely to work in some way alongside employees and for
mateship to be the model of workplace relationships. It is a style the
employer seeks to advance because the celebration of the common
worth of men blurs perceptions of class divisions and reduces the
potential for disharmony. It goes without saying that women are
absent from this scene.

Equality of opportunity

As Jayawardena points out, social equality is concerned with rights and opportunities. The trouble is, when we refer to equality of opportunity we do not all, and certainly not always, mean the same thing. Goldman distinguishes different senses of the concept (1979:170 *et seq*).

The first and, as he says, minimal sense is when positions or goods are allotted only on the basis of relevant performance and qualifications. His criticism here is that the approach is 'morally insufficient' unless in the first instance all people have equal chances to acquire the relevant qualifications and to develop their potential skills. In other words, it is not true equality of opportunity if some competitors come to the starting gate already socially handicapped.

The second sense is, therefore, expanded. The proposition is that people should be given the means of developing their 'natural potential' (however that may be identified and deemed relevant) and assisted in overcoming socially disadvantaging factors such as might be generated by their class, race or sex. It is thus a requirement of the social system that it offer a means of redress for the disadvantages it has imposed, recreated and often then amplified.

A third and more radical version of equality of opportunity builds on the second: we should take steps to correct not only for initial social disadvantages but also for natural disabilities. The reasoning behind this argument is 'that individuals no more deserve their natural than their social advantages' (Goldman 1979:174).

Again, the issue of just how many of Goldman's natural disabilities are really disguised forms of social disadvantage clouds the conceptual distinction between his second and third version of equality of opportunity. The mounting volume of evidence on the role that environmental and even cultural factors play in the incidence of birth defects is a case in point. Similarly, certain occupations are likely to result in a higher incidence of physical disability than others, and who has access to what occupations is directly related to questions of class, race and sex. This blurring inevitably raises questions of whether it is possible to set limits on the concept of equal opportunity and where it is socially and morally defensible to draw them in practice. It is also an invitation to confuse equality of outcome with equality of opportunity.

Yet it hardly seems unfair to support special facilities and programs for the physically or mentally handicapped. This is a matter of the allocation of public resources to allow all individuals to develop to their own full potential. It is not an attempt to even out differences in natural potential or all effects of differences in natural potential. What would attempts to homogenise society do to specially gifted or talented people and at what cost to society? Besides, the whole issue of equality of outcomes is tainted with a certain arrogance. Why should all people aspire to the same goals which will have been established as the most desirable goals of and by the socially dominant group and will most certainly accord benefits differentially among social groups? A cartoon produced in the early days of the Women's Liberation Movement gives pithy comment to this: on the question of seeking equality with men, the feminist response was, 'Actually we were hoping for something better.'

It is important to stress here, and whenever possible, that to seek to provide individuals with equal chances of benefits through natural capacity and effort is quite different from seeking to achieve proportionate representation of various social groups within employment or educational categories which are stamped desirable (see Goldman, 1979:183).

Fundamentally there are two arguments in support of equality. On the one hand it is advocated on the grounds of social justice and the rights of individuals. On the other hand there is the argument of utility.

Social rights, as just social claims and dues, are not absolute. This is no less true of their obverse—social responsibilities. They are hitched to social values and social structures; they are part of any social system. As such they are relative and subject to change. Some rights are enshrined in laws, others in moral codes varying in the degree to which they are unlikely or likely to be made law and in the degree to which they are likely or unlikely to encourage adherence. It is only relatively recently that equality of employment opportunity has been a consideration on the social and political agenda, and even more recently that steps were taken in some places to give it legal status.

As members of society we have rights to hold certain beliefs and receive social benefits, to behave in certain ways and even to hold various forms of property however broadly defined. Discounting social/legal obligations, we also possess rights not to have these things or perform in these ways. To have such rights and to exercise them (or not) is a basic form of social justice. But the social sands, on which individually identifiable rights rest, shift. Thus certain social arrangements can change from being unquestioned and/or acceptable to being perceived as wrong. Further, as Broom (1984:xxiv) questions in relation to gender, how are perceptions to be translated into behaviour once a social arrangement comes to be seen as unjust? She points to a number of difficulties bedevilling moves to change behaviour. These include the fact that majority opinion may have little immediate structural impact, pressure groups may unintentionally subvert the reform they seek, that it is unwise to assume any security in legal gains and that some forms of change (for instance, affirmative action) will in themselves generate hostility.

The truth of it is that having social justice responsive to change and working in practice is a very slow business (while history is strewn with this information, look particularly to the struggle of Aboriginal people since white settlement for fair treatment in their own land — Rowley, 1972; and to the question of women and welfare in Australia — Baldock and Cass, 1983). It is also somewhat elusive insofar as, by definition, social process, and therefore social justice as practice, is not static. Further, for these reasons, but also because in liberal democracy compromise is the essence of political pragmatism, social justice is usually wanting in its application. Despite all cautions, the notion is morally compelling and something of a social imperative; after all, the recognition of rights is sometimes the only bulwark against opposed and clamant interests.

Utilitarian arguments may harness notions of rights and social justice, but they may also be shy of them. Broad-based arguments for the utility of equality of opportunity refer to the achievement of more harmonious relationships between social groups in the society (Goldman, 1979:141−4). The claim is that by integrating differentiated and disadvantaged groups in the society tensions are eased or, to use the more recently developed rationale of certain sections of the Australian polity, 'social cohesion' is increased.

This occurs because in the breaking down of group consciousness previously volatile divisions become blurred and presumably disappear. Hence those in dominant positions cease to feel threatened and, insofar as dominated peoples no longer experience their frustrations, they cease to be threatening. We might, however, well question whether the aim is integration or assimilation — that is, whether the objective is the social incorporation of 'minority' groups while acknowledging their right to retain and assert their cultural differences, or an incorporation which requires relinquishing of cultural differences. If the proposed road to accord is by means of reducing group consciousness we are really looking at assimilation. Assimilation certainly seems to be the method by which social cohesion is to be achieved. But Aboriginal peoples, migrants and women are hardly likely to accede to a system in which esteemed characteristics, qualities and cultural forms distinguishing them from other social sets are discounted. Such homogenising would be very heavy-handed and patently unfair. But the idea of integration, in the sense of retaining difference without devaluation, no doubt always carries a challenge to existing hierarchies. Thus the whole issue of socially equal incorporation, as well as the means taken to achieve it, may generate more friction. Evidence of the backlash is clear enough (Broom, 1984:xxiv; Goldman, 1979:143). There is also the disutility of the possible unfair stigmatisation of those people who have achieved under equal opportunity policies (Goldman, 1979:144; Fishkin, 1983:93).

Narrower utilitarian arguments are couched in the context of efficiency. This appears to be particularly telling advocacy because it has direct relevance to individual organisations and sits at the centre of the ethos of production.

No-one could deny the efficiency of seeking the best person for the project — whatever it is. And it is true that so long as only some social categories are perceived as providing the catchment for recruitment of people to education and employment, then much potential talent is bound to be overlooked. What is disturbing is the way in which equality of opportunity has become an issue of efficiency. It is common to hear it defended in management terms and often only in those terms. The idea of social justice may sometimes be included but, as we illustrate later, it is as much a rider as anything else. This transformation has implications running counter to equality.

The quest for efficiency takes place within a given social framework. But social structure is fundamentally biased for it works in the established interests of already dominant groups. We are then faced with the likelihood that equality of opportunity, implemented according to criteria of efficiency, will be specifically directed to improving the chances of members of some social groups and not others who, for the very reasons of their initial structural disadvantage, will be less able to seize the opportunities. Thus basic inequalities are not challenged but rather endorsed. The charge that middle-class women stand to benefit over working-class men, let alone over working-class women who scarcely even get a look-in, may not be dismissed simply (see Goldman, 1979:197).

Utilitarian arguments cannot provide the reason for instituting equality of opportunity practices. This motivation must emanate from recognition of the need and the desire for social justice, set against the knowledge that the social structure itself is unequal and unjust. The question of efficiency is not, however, outcast because, while social justice is the prime mover, utility is likely to be an important and ultimate outcome.

Equity

Arguments for equity shadow discussions of equality and justice. It is as well to look more closely at the relationship to save confounding the concepts. In her analysis of equity Pateman draws attention to its distinguishing characteristics; it is, she points out, to do with general rules, not actual circumstances — it is a procedural notion. Essentially, it relates to the distribution of goods and services among individuals. The points of reference for ensuring that procedures are equitable lie in existing social structures. While the notion of equity is useful in examining Béteille's distributive aspect of inequality, it does not bear on the relational dimension which is, after all, fundamental. This structural fix is really the nub of Pateman's analysis, for 'although equity focuses on the criteria for distributing goods and services and on the fairness of rules governing liberal democratic institutions, the question never asked outside the political sphere is: who makes the rules?' (1981:35). It is all very well to push for equity in distributive systems but 'so long as wider interpretations of justice and equity are excluded, appeals to equity are ultimately useful primarily to those concerned to defend a fundamentally unequal and unjust social structure' (1981:36).

Kingston (1981) also takes up the considerations of equality and equity but turns the discussion differently. She argues that while questions of equity have not been historically relevant to women in Australia, they are increasingly becoming so. Theoretically women have achieved equality in a number of important areas. Her examples include the institutional political arena, the equal pay issue and the realm of sexuality. But she points out that legal and technical equality in no way assure effective equality. For this reason, she believes that once formal gains towards equality have been made, the positive and moderate demands of equity may be more useful in improving women's participation in society and their fair access to social benefits.

For all that the two approaches appear divergent there is good fit. We certainly need to recognise that structural bias and inequality render equity an illusory notion. But we must also heed the evidence that even given formal equality, people may be thwarted in actually enjoying it — thus recalling arguments for equity. At the level of theory and practice equality of opportunity relies on both sets of considerations. It is, of course, no new discovery that 'only against the background of a just basic structure, including a just political constitution and a just arrangement of economic and social institutions, can one say that the requisite procedure exists' (Rawls, 1972:87). But given the frequently pious and apparently exclusive commitment to the efficacy and adequacy of a limited range of formal procedures in reducing inequality it is obviously important to state this fact clearly and often.

Equal opportunity in employment

In the field of employment, equality of opportunity has been tied specifically to access to the labour market and to income and status returns (Moir, 1984:94). It focuses on market place barriers (see Wertheim, 1985).

The practices followed in recruitment, selection and appointment, promotion and the award of employment benefits, although varying from one organisation to another, are believed to be adequately documented or well enough known and patterned to be documented. No doubt for this reason income and status returns are the dimensions of employment which have attracted the most conspicuous efforts in pursuing equitable treatment for all job applicants and employees. If, however, the aim really is to achieve equality, review and reformist approaches will be superficial and inadequate unless account is taken of unwritten and often unacknowledged features of those very employment processes. For, like all other social behaviours, these formal or informal but institutionalised policies and/or practices have been developed and pursued on the basis of values and assumptions anchored in the wider social structure which is biased in the interests of certain classes of people. When, for example, it comes to the unconsidered but not inconsiderable weight of domestic commitments, women do not enter wage labour on the same terms as men; no more do socio-economically disadvantaged people participate with the same likelihood of success as those in more favoured class relationships.

In New South Wales, the first Australian state to enact Equal Employment Opportunity legislation, government departments, statutory authorities and institutions of tertiary education are obliged, as part of a management plan, to undertake a review of the spread of personnel practices. The reviews should cover recruitment and selection, staff training and development, promotion and transfer as well as conditions of service. The purpose is to reveal discriminatory practices.

The problem is that employers lacking goodwill may comply with the letter but not the spirit of the legislation and by ignoring underlying attitudes and informal conduct ensure that little meaningful change is made. It is a problem echoed in other proactive anti-discrimination legislation in Australia.

A criticism of Equal Employment Opportunity in the United States makes exactly this charge. The claim is that although what appear to be appropriate affirmative action gestures are often made they are really to satisfy compliance reviews or for public relations purposes and have little substance. They can, in effect, be merely window dressing (Benokraitis and Feagin, 1978:83).

A focus on personnel practices gives us something of the broad picture of the difficulties which members of particular social categories and groups experience in employment. It also provides a better idea of how individual organisations work. Fairer practices are more likely to be advocated and instituted in the light of such understanding. Yet, while this focus draws out some of the methods in which, say, horizontal segmentation of the labour market is maintained, it is not revealing of the more fundamental and discriminatory ways in which it is affirmed and protected. It takes no account, for example, of the fact that the sexual division of labour allocates work in the domestic sphere and in wage work, as well as between home and workplace (Game and Pringle, 1983:14−24; Baldock, 1983:22−25). Nor can it consider the relationships between class position and race or ethnic group (see de Lepervanche, 1980:33−35) and the direct implications of this relationship for segmentation of the labour force (Reich *et al*, 1980), which most certainly cements all manner of social disadvantage.

There is, too, the question of segregation of the labour market. Australia has long had a high level of occupational segregation by sex (Power, 1975) and occupational segregation generally is slow to break down (OECD, 1984). In class, race and sex terms, and for structural and attitudinal reasons, career choices have been limited. Occupational segregation not only signifies separation of fields of work, it limits them. The result is evident in job clustering and crowding for women, Aboriginal people and certain migrant groups who are to be found in disproportionately large numbers in a small set of occupations usually characterised by low average earnings, truncated career prospects, limited benefits and some costs in terms of occupational health and safety. Thus occupational segregation confirms social groups in positions of inequality and unequal opportunities.

Really, questions of access to the labour market must logically be raised both prior to and concurrently with the question of income and status returns. It becomes, as we have pointed out, a shallow exercise to press for equity if this is to be set against a social backdrop of inequality.

Discrimination

To discriminate against a person is to deny them equality of opportunity. It also prevents them from enjoying just and proper outcomes. As a concept discrimination is not necessarily well understood, as behaviour it is not necessarily clearly perceived. Not surprisingly, the tendency is to disclaim its occurrence or to avow that if once it occurred it is now eliminated. Individuals may resist the idea that it could (or does) happen to them because of the possibility of contagion, that is, a fear of having attributed to them some of the stereotyped qualities of the subject group. It goes without saying that these qualities are derogated in the dominant value system. Paradoxically it may be more comfortable to recognise one's position of disadvantage not as an individual but as a class, in which case the emphasis is likely to be on the admirable qualities of the class (Jayawardena, 1968). There is also the consideration that unless individuals — as subjects or agents of discrimination — acknowledge the injustice of it, then they are unlikely to observe discrimination in operation and will certainly not seek change. People seem better able, and probably more willing, to recognise discrimination the more they distance their sights. The pattern of the presbyopic response is aptly described in the setting of a university and when it relates to women as being something like this:

> it happens to women outside the university more than it does to women who work in universities and it happens to women in other departments more than in mine, and it happens to other women in my department more than it does to me. (Wills, 1983:113)

Individual members of dominant groups strongly resist any suggestion that they might be discriminatory, at the least because of the threat of moral censure and sometimes in anticipation of a stronger response, possibly to the extent of legal action.

Davies (1982:15 — 16) has set out a lucid classification of forms of discrimination which we follow here. She differentiates four levels. The first form is direct and intended discrimination. All parties recognise it. It occurs when, for whatever reason, action is purposefully taken to exclude a person from known benefits. It would include, for example, the refusal to employ Aboriginal labour on the basis of an argument recognised as racist but nonetheless advanced.

The second form, also direct but in this case unintended, occurs when the discriminator does not realise that invalid assumptions underlie actions with discriminatory outcomes. An example would be if a male applicant were chosen for a job over an equally well-qualified woman in the belief that men may resent working under or with her or that she would be less committed to forging a career.

In instances of indirect/structural discrimination, practices which appear to be neutral at face value are actually discriminatory. The practice of promotion by seniority, for instance, disadvantages women who do not notch up years of service at the same rate as men because of time taken out for bearing and caring for children. Similarly, superannuation benefits which are only fully payable after thirty years' continuous contribution to the scheme are discriminatory.

Finally, Davies says, there is systemic discrimination. It is an amalgam of the previous three forms which may both directly and indirectly decrease opportunities for women — and of course, for other socially disadvantaged groups. Moreover, systemic discrimination includes the lowered self-esteem and negative attitudes of self which people are likely to develop as a consequence of their continuing setbacks and struggles in a system of unequal opportunities.

Analysis of how discrimination is produced is essential to our understanding of it, but Abramson argues for the need to assess it in terms of outcomes.

> It matters not at all whether an employer wants to discriminate or has buried his prejudices so deeply that he innocently believes there is no discrimination whatever in his employment practices or even if he sincerely and honestly has no discriminatory intentions. What matters is where women and minorities are somehow victimized by those employment practices. (1979:25)

The point is that instigation and agency, whether intentional or unintentional, individual or structural, overt or covert, as well as processes and outcomes of discrimination, all need to be taken into account if we are to be able to see the way to justice with any clarity.

As Davies (1982) writes, the levels of discrimination are partly historical, being more direct and visible at the first level but increasingly complex and opaque in later forms. It is easy to identify overt and direct discrimination — the 'women and Blacks need not apply' syndrome. The reality is that discrimination is more likely to be invisible or structurally masked in its workings but attested in outcomes; for example in the under-representation of women and Aboriginal people in certain employment categories and positions. It is, however, important to be aware of the difficulties of assessing what representation might mean. For example, we cannot take under-representation in employment as proof of discrimination although it must surely alert us to that possibility (see Over, 1981). Even so, discriminatory attitudes and beliefs, while expressed systemically are not necessarily well disguised. Certainly since 1966 marriage has not automatically put paid to a career in the Commonwealth Public Service for women (it never did for men), but it other arenas 'protective' legislation has continued to debar women from certain occupations. Thornton (1983) cogently points out that it is unlawful to employ women in certain types of work if it requires them to lift weights of more than 16 kilograms or to mine underground. The expressed intention is to protect women from work deemed unsuitable. (The question is, who deems it so and why?) The effect, however, has been to restrict their employment. Moreover the contradictions of practice have been sidestepped: in domestic life women commonly hoist heavy weights — the children, shopping, furniture and so on — and certainly do so in the traditionally female field of nursing. And goodness knows how some men feel when their employment requires them to lift great weights; never mind that they are below average height, below average weight and possibly have a hernia. It is relevant that back injury is one of the most commonly occurring industrial injuries in the Australian male workforce.

Affirmative Action

Affirmative Action was formulated in response to the perceived in-adequacies of reactive non-discrimination. It represents a broadening of anti-discrimination goals and concomitant expansion of the means of achieving them. In Australia the term affirmative action is used only in reference to women and in this context is interchangeable with EEO. Affirmative Action and EEO constitute the means of achieving equality of opportunity.

There is, however, not simply one affirmative action approach to breaking down patterns of social inequality. Nor indeed is there virtue in orthodoxy. As Jewson and Mason (1986b) point out, there is a range of possible responses and actions extending from liberal to radical. Often enough in discussion and representation the range is conflated to just one stance, that is, the terms and concepts of liberal and radical debates are used in a 'confused, arbitrary and contradic-tory manner'. While this may indeed reflect a muddle and misunder-standing in thinking we cannot dismiss the suggestion that it can represent attempts to mislead and mystify (see Jewson and Mason, 1986b:308).

In its reactive form anti-discrimination legislation is really a cor-rective measure. It offers a means of resolving and redressing instances of discrimination experienced by individuals in groups covered by that legislation (Wilenski, 1977:231). A complaint-based system, reactive non-discrimination delineates the offence and allows in-dividual and easily identified transgressors to be picked off, but in-evitably it is narrow in approach, patchy in application and painfully slow in effecting change. If any corrective action is taken it is, and unfairly, the victims themselves who must instigate it. While such legislation is a necessary tool in breaking down discriminatory be-haviour it is not sufficient and certainly cannot cope with the bias and bent of systemic discrimination.

On the other hand affirmative action is intended to correct such systemic inequality and aims to channel responsibility away from individuals to bureaucratic and corporate roosts. It is premised on the need for organisations to initiate positive and coherent action to eliminate structural discrimination. The expression has its origins in the United States where since the sixties it has been controversial policy in employment and higher education (see Benokraitis and Feagin, 1978). Not until the seventies was it seriously considered in Australia—in 1977 Wilenski included it as a means of achieving necessary change in his interim report on the review of New South Wales Government administration (1977:231—242).

The term itself—affirmative action—jars the sensibilities of some but any irritation with the words pales next to the fiercely hostile reactions associated with, all too often, wilful misinterpretations and misapplications of them. Take, for example, Levin's address, 'Affirmative Action: Discrimination against men and their wives' (1984), which is peppered with simple-minded and distorting assertions such as:

> 'Affirmative action is the policy of preferring women to men' (8),
> 'affirmative action conflicts with merit' (8),
> 'For every woman who benefits from affirmative action against a man, another woman is penalized, namely, the wife of the man passed over.' (11)

and so on.

Without doubt the promise or threat of affirmative action has immediate effect in polarising attitudes. People are either for it or against it, and strongly so. Prior to its introduction indifference did not seem to register as an option. Neutrality here offered either no refuge or no appeal. The ayes are, not surprisingly, individuals or groups who find it unacceptable that categories of people have been made targets of discrimination on the basis of shared physical or social attributes with imputed debilitating consequences for social performance. They endorse not only the principles of equality of oppportunity but the practical features of affirmative action. They accept, say, special training programs for Aboriginal people, a requirement that there should be representation of women on selection committees and alterations to the built environment for the physically handicapped as some of the steps which must be taken (but by no means in isolation) towards breaking down patterns of disadvantage. Detractors display a more conservative disposition and are happy to endorse the *status quo*. They, either consciously or unconsciously, side-step or reject arguments that difference may politically, economically or in other social ways be turned to disadvantage. They hold that certain inequalities are given and are therefore not only irrefutable but acceptable and indeed necessary. They know, for instance, that women's relative disadvantage has a genetic basis. As an example, a letter published in *The Age* querulously asks

> When will we get an article which honestly admits that excellence and creativity at the higher levels in maths, chess and music composition are linked with male chromosomes, i.e. that men as a group outperform females as a group in these areas? (10.7.1984)

The reasoning of racism follows the same lines. For its detractors the notion of affirmative action threatens established order, thereby generating insecurity which confirms conservatism and sharpens criticism. The circularity inherent in this exposition merely reflects the circularity of the censor's reasoning. Of course, in this context we cannot overlook the issue of interest, but we deal with that more fully later. What is interesting is the development of indifference, evident after affirmative action policies and programs have been operating for a period of time. Strong voices may still be heard for and against, but possibly because it is neither as good nor as bad as first believed the silences increase. Is it apathy, passive acceptance or passive rejection?

Although the emphasis in affirmative action appears to be on redressing the legacy of past discrimination it is also aimed at, and indeed has the effect of, eliminating present discrimination and preventing its future occurrence. As Thornton (1984:120) observes, it is this eye to the future which distinguishes affirmative action measures from traditional legal remedies. While affirmative action has been a requirement of some anti-discrimination legislation, it need not be confined to legislative reform. A number of private sector corporations, independently of any demands the law made of them, moved to introduce affirmative action in one form or another. To just what degree such action was taken in anticipation of legislation, or quite independently of these considerations, is another matter.

Affirmative action is actually an umbrella term for a whole range of possible corrective responses to manifestations of discrimination. It is common knowledge that it involves reviewing the policies and practices of recruitment, selection and advancement in employment as well as the provision of employee benefits. The truth is that it can extend well beyond these measures and need bear no mark of preferential treatment. Among employment-related considerations, it also covers the provision of child care, offering special training courses, adjusting work and meeting timetables, recognising hitherto undervalued skills and capacities, making permanent part-time employment possible (without penalties) and addressing the problem of the differential rewards attending occupational segregation by sex, race or ethnic background. But it can go further; in education it might encompass rethinking who should study certain subjects, to what level, what might constitute the subject matter and even the form education might take. It would also have application in restructuring financial arrangements more equitably in fields such as superannuation and tax and transfer systems (see, for example, Bryson, 1983; Cass, 1983; Edwards, 1984; Roe, 1983). It has been significant in reviewing the law, as was apparent in the Conference on Legislative and Award Restrictions to Women's Employment held in Canberra in October 1986. For Aboriginal people it certainly applies to the question of land rights. And the list does not end there. The trouble is that while in principle affirmative action expands the goals of anti-discrimination and the remedies to deal with the problem, the understanding and the practice of it are much more limited.

Principally affirmative action is seen as having to do with employment by relatively large employers (not even unemployment or under-employment), and especially with particular aspects of it. But, despite the central and crucial role of employment in a capitalist society, concentration on it does not have inevitable and automatic spillover to other dimensions of social process. They demand attention in their own right. We should certainly be examining disadvantaging processes. How is it that women generally are allocated social roles giving access to a lower level of benefits in the socially constructed hierarchy of good? How is it that Aboriginal people are excluded from the full benefits of citizenship? Clearly the vote is not the only entrée. By what means are migrants socially marginalised? And what of disabling processes? The tightness of focus of both critics and proponents suggests we are in danger of collapsing the potential of affirmative action to narrowed aims and disjunctive methods — part-grounds of the critique of reactive anti-discrimination offered by the advocates of affirmative action.

Dirty words

If the term affirmative action is beleaguered, then a quick dip into just some of the literature, or a brief chat with a marplot, is enough to identify other words groaning under a pejorative overload — even though the burden is frequently misplaced.

'Target' is just such a word. The *Macquarie Dictionary* offers a simple and fitting definition for these purposes — 'a goal to be reached'. The goal may be broad, such as the elimination of discriminatory elements — sexism in personnel practices, or racism in school curricula. On the other hand it may be a specific target, such as formulating non-discriminatory guidelines for interviewing candidates for jobs, or the removal of sexist language from school primers or university bylaws. Little hostility seems to be generated by broadly defined goals. It is a different matter at more specific levels. The threat of change, which may then be interpreted as a threat to individual interests, crystallises.

The use of the word target also appears in the term 'target group'. Target groups are those who are supposed to be the beneficiaries of moves toward equal opportunity in employment, the disadvantaged group specifically identified in EEO and Affirmative Action legislation as deserving of particular attention. Just which groups are so identified varies from one piece of legislation to the next and changes over time. The physically disabled, for example, became a target group for the New South Wales legislation only in 1984. Regrettably, many affirmative action measures are quite literally, to use another definition of target offered by the *Macquarie Dictionary*, 'fixed at or aimed at' these specifically identified groups. For example, rather than have employers create work environments in which less 'assertive' employees can be productive and prosper, members of disadvantaged groups are sent off to assertiveness training sessions.

Some particular goals are quantifiable and quantified — numerical targets in the jargon of affirmative action. These stimulate phobic responses and perhaps for no other reason than that (a very good one) should be used with extreme circumspection and only if really necessary.

Forward estimates or numerical targets are percentages, or even raw numbers which the organisation concerned believes it can realistically meet, in appointments, promotions, etc. over a specific period, the intention being to improve the presence and chances of an unfairly under-represented group. Forward estimates or numerical targets are set voluntarily by organisations, taking into account their own structure and needs. They are not externally enforceable and they may be subject to adjustment. But, for reasons of misunderstanding or mischief, they are confused with quotas more often than not.

The bogey of quotas stalks discussions of affirmative action:

> As I was going up the stair
> I met a man who wasn't there!
> He wasn't there again today!
> I wish, I wish he'd go away!*

Quotas are numerical requirements in hiring. There may be externally imposed sanctions on failure to meet them. There is, however, no reason quotas should constitute the concern they do; indeed

---

* from 'Antigonish' by Hughes Mearns, 1922

for some it is an obsession. They are not, and have not been, proposed in the Australian context. Yet the spectre of quotas is raised time and again and, with some prestidigitation, presented as a contentious issue. Even in the United States, their country of origin, they are not a requirement of the executive orders dealing with affirmative action. It is true set quotas have occasionally, but only occasionally, been imposed by federal courts in the United States. But this has only been after a specific finding of glaring and persistent discrimination. Benokraitis and Feagin call the outcry against quotas, with its overtones of a rallying crusade, phoney (1978:173).

Preferential treatment is often seen simply and superficially as reverse discrimination. Discussion of it usually pitches in to vitriolic debate. In broad terms preferential treatment is viewed as a form of compensation for the cumulative disadvantages of past discrimination. It means favouring members of certain social categories over other competitors to neutralise historic discrimination. The supporting argument is that unless it is practised, structural bias prevails and those persons already advantaged by the system will continue to be the beneficiaries of systemic injustice (Sher, 1977:52).

The terms preferential treatment (which includes the more specific preferential hiring) and reverse discrimination are nonetheless highly problematical, whether they are used indiscriminately and interchangeably (see, for example Cohen, Nagel and Scanlon, 1977; Goldman, 1979) or whether preferential treatment is seen as the practice resulting in reverse discrimination. Counteraction of the effects of discrimination is, after all, the very reason for invoking corrective measures.

The issue of individual fairness arises when reverse discriminatory processes bypass individuals, not for reasons of lesser qualification but on the basis of unalterable characteristics not related to performance (as with systemic discrimination). Goldman argues that: 'Having unwittingly benefited from acts of injustice may create a liability to compensate them, at least to the degree of relinquishing undeserved benefits, but it does not generally imply any guilt for the acts' (1979:108).

The attribution of individual guilt is neither useful nor possible and is certainly no justification of reverse discrimination. The emergent problem is not structural, the approach is simply not fair. But while the question of guilt is generally accepted as misconceived, the issue of a collective liability which can be vitiated through reverse discrimination remains essentially contested. Leaving aside any quarrels with the principle, the fact remains that with reverse discrimination the collective liability is discharged through individuals. Sher, however, claims that to object to an uneven distribution of the burden of compensation among some individuals misses the point:

> The crucial fact about these individuals is not that they are more
> *responsible* for past discrimination than others with relevantly
> similar histories..., but rather that unless reverse discrimination
> is practiced, they will *benefit* more than the others from its effects
> on their competitors. (1977:54−5)

Nagel, in the same publication (1977), writes that while forms of
compensatory treatment are not a requisite of justice, they are not
incompatible with it and concludes they are 'probably not unjust'.

Whatever moral justifications are advanced for compensatory treatment, the mere suggestion of it carries considerable costs in criticism.
As Thornton suggests (1984:125), it is therefore desirable to focus on
corrective rather than compensatory action. But it is important to see
that the term preferential treatment is used in two ways. For some, it
is directly translated as reverse discrimination, or at least has that as
an outcome. Given the moral problems raised, this is a difficult approach to defend. Preferential treatment may also, however, be used
in a narrower and less contentious sense. The suggestion here is not
that lesser qualified people should succeed over better qualified competitors (the usual chorus of objection) but that, given equally qualified
candidates, preference should be accorded to members of social categories of people identified as subjects of discrimination. While still
aimed at obvious symptoms of discrimination rather than the social
processes producing it, such action is justified on the grounds that it is
a necessary means of intervening in the re-creation of systemic bias. In
this sense we are not speaking of a compensatory step (that is neither
the intention nor the outcome) but rather of corrective action. The
aim is to correct the skew in the allocation of present and future
benefits.

2

Background

Being a discussion of the experience of the United States of America in legislating for equal employment opportunity: the requirements, their impact and the problems. And a discussion of the background to the development of similar legislation in Australia.

Why the path the USA travelled in search of equal opportunity in employment was chosen as the one Australia should follow, despite a very different political culture and labour traditions, no doubt reflects the glaring visibility of the USA to Australian reformers. As the secretary to Mel Semblar, George Bush's nominee for the position of Ambassador to Australia, said in comment on what made Australia an attractive posting to her boss, 'Australia is an American speaking country' (1989). There are different examples of how the problems of unequal pay, labour market segmentation and segregation have been, and are being, handled by countries like Sweden, which has labour traditions more similar to our own—but Sweden is not an American speaking country (see O'Donnell and Hall, 1988).

The experience of the United States

The requirements for non-discrimination, equal employment opportunity and affirmative action in the United States derive from a multiplicity of sources:
- From legislation, some of it dating back to last century, for example, the Civil Rights Act of 1866, the Civil Rights Act of 1871, the Equal Pay Act of 1963, Title VII of the Civil Rights Act of 1964, Age Discrimination in Employment Act of 1967, Rehabilitation Act of 1973, Vietnam Era Veterans Readjustment Act of 1974;
- From Presidential Directives, such as Executive Orders 11246, 11141, 11625, 12138; and
- From a growing body of case law from courts in several jurisdictions, most notably the United States Supreme Court.

The grounds of discrimination made unlawful by these requirements are race, colour, religion, sex, national origin, age, physical and

19

mental handicap, Vietnam veteran status and majority group member status. Affirmative Action in particular is required for Blacks, Hispanics, American Indians, orientals, women, religious minorities, handicapped persons, disabled veterans and Vietnam veterans. One estimate puts the proportion of the population covered by various programs for the disadvantaged at something approaching 70 per cent (McGuiness, 1988).

Employment practices that are deemed unlawful are outright direct discrimination, unintentional discrimination, practices with discriminatory consequences (disparate impact, subjective evaluations and reliance on stereotypes, chilling) and passive acceptance of discrimination. Which employers are covered depends upon the particular source of the requirement: subsidiaries of foreign-owned multinationals, labour unions, businesses which affect commerce and need at least 15 workers each work day in each of 20 or more calendar weeks in the current or preceding year. State and local governments are covered by non- or anti-discrimination legislation; federal government, educational institutions accepting federal funds, and contractors and subcontractors having contracts with the federal government (depending on the size of the workforce and the value of the contract) are covered by equal employment opportunity and affirmative action requirements. And, until 1978, when Jimmy Carter tried to rationalise the system for administering equal employment opportunity programs, twenty-one separate agencies were responsible for the administration, monitoring and enforcement of employment discrimination laws. Since 1978, the courts, the office of Federal Contracts Compliance and the Equal Employment Opportunity Commission (EEOC) share responsibility for administering the programs. Other departments, especially the Justice Department, have responsibility for enforcement (Bryner, 1981:416−417). CCH's *Guidebook to Fair Employment Practices* is almost 200 pages long and is described in the foreword as 'a brief explanatory course through the numerous laws and regulations' (1983:3). There are the more usual statutory exemptions to the requirements but one has a distinctively American flavour − 'the federal bans on race, color, religion, sex and national origin bias do not apply with respect to the employment of aliens outside the United States, or to Communists' (CCH, 1983:34). The requirements are numerous, complex, and appear to be far reaching. For example, an observer who passively accepts or acquiesces in the discrimination of another is guilty of forbidden discrimination. Moreover unions may be implicated in discrimination by virtue of being party to a contract. If under a negotiated contract there is any discrimination, the union is accountable, whether or not it is aware of the practices (CCH, 1983:32).

The enforcement sanctions appear to be powerful enough — withdrawal of federal funds, disruption to business through withdrawal of federal contracts, long and costly fights in the courts with the threat of spectacular settlements such as that awarded against American Telephone and Telegraph in 1973: $US15 million in back pay for 13 000 female employees to compensate them for past discrimination (Robinson, 1979:431). Most recently, in January 1989, the Harris Trust and Savings Bank, without admitting to having discriminated against its employees, agreed to pay $US14 million to women and minorities it employed (but failed to promote) between 1974 and 1986. As many as 5000 people could be involved in the settlement. The case ran for 15 years, much longer than the resources of complainants usually last (*Off Our Backs*, Feb. 1989:4).

Measuring effectiveness

Diprete and Soule draw attention to the substantial literature on the socioeconomic progress of women and minorities since World War II. They ask whether equal employment opportunity legislation and policies have had any effect here, but can find no clear answer. Some writers find positive outcomes, others see no significant effect while others draw what are described as 'mixed' conclusions (1986:295).

The first difficulty in determining whether EEO/AA programs have achieved anything derives from the impossibility of isolating those programs from other programs and from general movements. If change (using whatever indices we might agree on) has occurred we can never say that it was the result of the AA programs and those programs alone. The other difficulty, of course, is reaching agreement on indices of change — changes in what? Do we look for changes in numbers employed and employed at particular levels in particular organisations? Do we look for reductions in salary differentials? Do we look for signs of a breaking down of labour market segregation and segmentation? Or, seeing AA programs as a means to a broader end (rather than an end in itself), do we look for changes in economic wellbeing, moves toward a more just society?

One of the reasons for the different assessments of the effectiveness of Affirmative Action Programs in the United States lies precisely in the use of different indices of success. In 1983, for example, the *New York Times* headlined a story, 'Study Says Affirmative Action Rule Expands Hiring Minorities' (Pear, June 1983). Chertos, in 1984, wrote: 'The objectives of affirmative action have not been met. This is a hard truth. Moreover, the objectives of affirmative action are not likely to be fully met within the foreseeable future. This is an even harder truth.' (1984:231).

By and large, claims for the success of the US Affirmative Action Program come from analyses of changes in the numbers appointed and/or promoted in individual organisations or a small number of organisations, that is, a small unit of analysis with a fairly narrowly defined indicator of success (see, for example, Bocher, 1982; Clynch and Gaudin, 1982; Hitt and Keats, 1984; Stewart and Bullock, 1981). If, however, we set only marginally broader goals for the programs, then pay differentials, labour market segregation and segmentation and the like, appear to have remained remarkably resistant to them.

Looking only at the two major groups the US programs originally covered — Blacks and women — the lack of major changes to these groups and some of the unintended consequences of small changes become depressingly obvious. For example, while the proportion of Black households making over $US50 000 a year rose from 4.5 per cent in 1970 to 8.8 per cent in 1986, the number of Black households making less than $US10 000 a year rose by 11 per cent. And Black families are four times more likely than whites to have incomes below the official poverty line (Hacker, 1987). Changes in the position of Black women appear to be crucial in changes at both ends of the economic spectrum. For example, the 11 per cent increase in the number of Black households below the poverty line is largely attributable to the increase in the number of such families headed by women. Note that 36 per cent of white women who head households fall into the poverty group compared with 56 per cent of Black women.

Since 1950, the average weekly wages of Black men have risen from 55 per cent to 73 per cent of white earnings, but Black employment rates have dropped: in 1954 more than 75 per cent of Black men were working full time all year round; in 1986, only 40 per cent were (Hacker, 1987). In many areas more Black women are employed than Black men. For example, Black women (who are more likely than Black men to complete college) account for· 66 per cent of all professional positions held by Blacks. Among white professionals women hold 48 per cent of the jobs. And Black women earn better, relatively, than their white counterparts. A Black man with four years of college earns $US784 for every $US1000 his white counterpart earns; a Black woman with four years college earns $US1017 for every $US1000 earned by her white counterpart. Just how much of this can be attributed to specific affirmative action programs is arguable. As Hacker (1987) comments:

> Organisations tend to have images of the qualities they want in their employees, and insofar as these models build on "white" attitudes and traits, it becomes harder for blacks to come across as qualified for openings and promotions. I am not referring here to such basic standards as literacy and reliability, but rather to the

doubts of white employers about how well blacks fit into the social settings of "white" offices and factories. (I have placed quotation marks around "white", because Asians seem to have had little trouble in satisfying these doubts.) And. . .it would appear that black women are better able to pass such tests than black men. At issue here are institutional expressions of racism.

For some employers, Black men appear to be much blacker than Black women. One area seems particularly resistant to Black employment — the financial industries. According to Rothschilds it is in finance, insurance and real estate that Blacks and Hispanics have the lowest industrial representation, except for mining. In the fastest growing occupation, 'sales representatives, securities and financial services', 70 per cent of employees are white males, fewer than 2 per cent are Black (1988).

Blacks as well as women in the US are heavily dependent on government employment. Rothschilds breaks up the approximately 12 million new jobs created during the Reagan administration into four major categories:

- 2 million in services to wealth or to the rich: finance, real estate, insurance and legal services. These are the best paid jobs and very few of these new jobs went to Blacks or Hispanics.
- 3.1 million in the semi-private welfare society: health, education and social services dependent on government programs. These went largely to women (and some to Blacks) and were accompanied by an expansion in poorly paid jobs and an increase in poverty.
- 3.8 million 'poverty jobs': cooks, sales clerks in the retail trade and hotels with short job tenure and very low benefits. These are the jobs that went to Blacks, Hispanics and illegal immigrants.
- 2.3 million jobs in construction, trucking and handling. Physically demanding and dangerous, almost half went to Black and Hispanic men (Rothschilds, 1988).

More generally, the median value of net worth for white households with assets in 1984 was \$US39 135; for Black households with assets, it was \$US3 397.

Hacker (1986) estimates that between 1980 and 1986 almost 80 per cent of new jobs created went to women. In 1960 only 35 per cent of American women were in the labour force. In 1986 the figure was 55 per cent with women holding 44 per cent of all jobs. The largest single source of new workers has been married women: in 1960, 19 per cent of married women with children were in the labour force; by 1986, 54 per cent of them were. Over the same time period, however, the time husbands devoted to family tasks increased by only 6 per cent (Hacker, 1986). Those women have by and large entered 'traditional women's jobs' (see Table 2.2). A National Research Council study has estimated that 'the overall degree of sex segregation...has not changed much since at least 1900' (cited in Hacker, 1986). This goes part way to explaining why women as a group in 1984 still made only $US637 for every $US1000 earned by men (see Table 2.1). What gains women have made may be illusory and, in the longer term, costly. For example, one of the most visible areas, certainly in terms of advertising if nothing else, has been the 'women into management' push. Executive employment in the US since 1973 has grown faster than total employment. For women, the increase has been at a rate of 8.6 per cent per annum and for men 2.1 per cent per annum. But not only are women executives concentrated in low paid

Table 2.1 Jobs and gender: women's versus men's earnings 1984 (US)

	Average weekly earnings	Percentage women	Earnings per $1,000 for men
Best-paid women			
Lawyers	$576	20.2%	$878
Engineers	$486	5.9%	$828
Computer analysts	$454	29.4%	$780
Most poorly paid women			
Cashiers	$164	80.9%	$816
Farm workers	$153	12.7%	$841
Waiters	$152	82.8%	$724
"Women's occupations"			
Secretaries & typists	$250	98.5%	$735
Registered nurses	$402	94.4%	$998
Information clerks	$221	88.6%	$726
"Men's occupations"			
Security guards	$217	11.1%	$882
Engineers	$486	5.9%	$828
Mechanics & repairers	$326	3.1%	$886
Highest earnings ratio			
Registered nurses	$402	94.4%	$998
Postal clerks	$407	32.2%	$923
Packers & packagers	$207	66.4%	$888
Lowest earnings ratio			
Financial managers	$359	38.7%	$627
Marketing & advertising managers	$367	21.0%	$598
Production inspectors	$220	53.1%	$553

Source: Bureau of Labor Statistics, cited in Hacker, 1986

occupations, there has also been a good deal of title inflation and a concomitant decline in the relative positions of executives. After all, in the US nowadays, one worker in eight is classified as an 'executive, administrator or manager' (Hacker, 1986). Just to prove that every silver lining has a cloud, a study by the National Academy of Sciences showed that as women enter a field earnings tend to drop, not only for themselves but for the men who remain too. Each time women rose by a percentage point in an occupation, the field as a whole fell $US42 in median annual earnings (cited in Hacker, 1986; see also Sokoloff, 1988).

Harding asks the following question of affirmative action programs designed to increase the number of women in science. The same question, and her answers, apply equally well to affirmative action programs in general:

Is it worthwhile expending the immense time, effort and agony necessary to carry out the affirmative action struggles when the root of the problem lies...in the organization of society's gender relations...?

Well, no and yes. No, because these strategies alone cannot create equity for women...Yes, because such action does bring small advances, change a few minds, make a little more space for future generations of women, create political consciousness and solidarity among women (and men) who struggle for equity, and reveal the nature of the beast through its forms of resistance to 'reasonable' demands. (Harding, 1986:247)

Table 2.2 Women's jobs and men's jobs

Mainly Women		Rarely Women	
Dental Hygienists	99.5%	Loggers	1.0%
Preschool Teachers	98.8%	Auto Mechanics	1.7%
Secretaries	98.4%	Tool and Die Makers	2.0%
Receptionists	97.6%	Skilled Building Trades	2.1%
Practical Nurses	96.9%	Millwrights	2.7%
Day-care Center Workers	96.1%	Stationary Engineers	2.7%
Domestic Servants	95.8%	Mechanical Engineers	3.7%
Typists	95.6%	Aircraft Mechanics	4.2%
Dressmakers	95.5%	Carpenters	4.4%
Registered Nurses	95.1%	Civil Engineers	4.7%
Dieticians	93.9%	Industrial Engineers	4.7%
Speech Therapists	93.8%	Welders and Cutters	4.8%
Teachers' Aides	93.6%	Machinists	5.2%
Bank Tellers	93.0%	Sheet-Metal Workers	5.2%

Sources: Bureau of Labour Statistics and National Center for Education Statistics, cited in Hacker, 1986

The nature of the beast revealed through its forms of resistance to reasonable demands may be part of the explanation for what appears to be a shift in emphasis of women's movement activity in the employment area in the US. Affirmative Action Programs have not come up with many of the goods some believed them capable of delivering, they still cost their intended beneficiaries enormously, and they can backfire. Even the Equal Employment Opportunity Commission (EEOC) stopped using numerical goals and timetables (as remedial tools) in employment discrimination settlements in 1985 because they had not worked (*Off Our Backs*, April 1986). More women's movement attention and energy has recently been devoted to comparable worth cases. The differences between the two approaches is important. In bald terms, affirmative action programs acknowledge that men occupy better paid jobs and seek to assist women to enter those jobs and earn better pay; they are assimilationist and clearly constitute 'reasonable' demands. But the beast has adapted well—by simply resisting or, where that is not possible, by changing its shape. By concentrating efforts on moving women (and others) into men's jobs affirmative action programs reinforce the high value ascribed to those jobs and the low value ascribed to the work traditionally performed by women.

Faith in affirmative action coincided with the dominance of the liberal-egalitarian strand in the movement—women wanted equality with men. That dominance has been challenged not only by the resistance of men to having women equal to them but also by another strand of thinking that has always been present in the women's movement and which does not want equality with men because so much of what men have is not worth having. Spurred on by the influence of French feminist philosophy's 'celebration of difference', by the failure of affirmative action and by the increasing pauperisation of women, this strand claims value for what women are and what women do. In the employment area, it seeks not to devalue further the work women have traditionally performed by encouraging them to leave it, but to value women's work properly and pay it accordingly. As Kessler-Harris argues; 'comparable worth calls for nothing less than the revaluation of women. Its strength lies in its potential for acting upon female traditions, for it assumes that women have a right to pursue traditional roles and to achieve equity in that pursuit' (1988:245).

A comparable worth approach takes two jobs and compares them by breaking each down into factors such as levels of skills, degrees of responsibility, expertise, effort and so on and seeks to have those factors scored and the total score paid. A crucial part of the exercise is to attach values to these factors. This is not unproblematical — for instance, responsibility for money, as for example in finance jobs, has traditionally attracted a higher point score than responsibility for lives, as for example in nursing (but presumably not in doctoring).

The initial flurry of activity in comparable worth cases in the US has resulted in the same spectacular settlements as did early sex discrimination and affirmative action decisions. By March 1986 one estimate of the amount of comparable worth gains made by workers, women workers in the main, put the figure at $US200 million (*Off Our Backs*, March 1986). The Alaska State Commission for Human Rights, for example, ruled that the state violated its own equal pay legislation, by not paying its predominantly female public health nurses the same as it paid its all male physicians' assistants when both groups performed 'work of comparable character' on the criteria of skill, responsibility, effort and working conditions. To rectify that injustice could cost the state $US1.5 million in back pay and interest to a group of 70 nurses. San Francisco City has worked out a $US8.8 million comparable worth plan for city employees (*Off Our Backs*, March 1986); the City of Chicago a plan that will cost the city around $US1.2 million a year for three years; the State of Wisconsin a plan estimated to cost $US9.1 million; and the State of Iowa one that will cost $US19 million over four years. Negotiated salary adjustments have awarded $US12 million to clerical and library workers in Los Angeles, $US5.6 million to 9000 Connecticut employees, $US36 million for New York State employees and $US40 million for 9000 Minnesota employees. But like early sex discrimination and affirmative action decisions, comparable worth settlements are being challenged every inch of the way up through the US court system. One of the largest comparable worth decisions of $US500−$US800 million in the State of Washington was overturned on appeal to the courts. Rather than spend more years pursuing the claim up the court hierarchy, an out of court settlement was reached which involved the state paying out $US46.5 million to correct wage inequities over 1986−87 with an additional $US10 million a year each year between 1987 and 1992 to complete the process (*Off Our Backs*, February 1986).

But the comparable worth track, while revealing more about the nature of the beast and making some gains, does not contain 'the answer' any more than affirmative action does. Debate among American feminists over the radical potential (or lack thereof) of comparable worth is vigorous. Kessler-Harris, for example, argues that comparable worth, in equating female and male workers, would threaten the men's sense of worth and offer a challenge to basic (masculine) institutions (1988:245). Brenner, on the other hand, warns not only of its limitations but also of its potential to increase 'racial and occupational divisions among working women' and 'exacerbate hierarchies in women's jobs' (1987:458–459; see also Steinberg, 1987:466–475). Comparable worth campaigns will undoubtedly reveal more of the nature of the beast and its ability to transform itself when prodded. Chances are, however, that Barbara Reskin's explanation for wage disparity will become increasingly difficult to resist: 'In sum, the basic cause of the income gap is not sex segregation but men's desire to preserve their advantaged position and their ability to do so by establishing rules to distribute valued resources in their favour' (1988:61).

The problems with affirmative action — US style

Bryner reports that in January 1979 Sears, Roebuck & Company filed a complaint in the federal district court in Washington DC against ten federal agencies with responsibility for administering equal employment policies in the United States. The charges related to the conflicting requirements in federal employment laws, the failure to take proper steps to provide a diverse workforce, the failure to develop adequate statistical data for purposes of comparison and for fostering discrimination within the federal government. What Sears called for was coordination in the enforcement of anti-discrimination statutes and uniformity in guidelines instructing employers how to resolve conflicts between existing and new affirmative action requirements (1981:411). The case was dismissed by the court but the complaint reveals some of the difficulties the Americans have experienced with their programs.

Sex was added to the 1964 Civil Rights Bill late in the Congressional debate as an attempt to have the whole Bill, concerned with race, defeated. It did not work and before very long complaints of sex discrimination began to mount. The swamping of bureaucratic agencies designated to handle the ever expanding requirements for non-discrimination and affirmative action became a feature common to all the agencies. For example, by June 1973 the Equal Employment Opportunity Commission backlog was estimated to include over 65 000 uninvestigated complaints (Robinson, 1979:431); further, by June 1976 there were 1400 sex discrimination complaints filed with Health, Education and Welfare not investigated and 800 unanswered letters (Chisholm, 1979:511); the Labor Department, responsible for monitoring affirmative action programs and compliance by companies doing business with the governmment, had to monitor the affirmative action programs of approximately 105 000 companies (*Business Week*, 1984:144).

There were also some singularly inappropriate designations. Health, Education and Welfare (HEW), for example, whose traditional role was to look after educational and welfare institutions, was also charged with requiring them to comply with affirmative action programs. In 1974, a number of women's organisations filed suit against HEW in the Washington Federal District Court. The Women's Equity Action League, the National Organization for Women, the National Education Association, the Federation of Organizations for Professional Women and the Association of Women in Science charged HEW with a whole range of derelictions related to affirmative action responsibilities (Abramson, 1976:185). HEW claimed lack of staff, the intended beneficiaries of the programs claimed lack of will.

For employers the requirements have meant the expenditure of large amounts of resources trying to comply with conflicting requirements by producing mountains of paper, filing only marginally different returns with different bureaucratic agencies. For the agencies it has meant overload, jurisdictional battles with each other, and being taken to court by their clients as well as by employers. For those whom the legislation was intended to benefit, even though the affirmative action provisions were meant to shift the burden of proof from discriminated to discriminator, it has meant a continuing struggle through the bureaucratic maze and into the courts.

In what one commentator has called a 'classic piece of American law', employers and employees were invited to continue their fights over employment in a series of political arenas increasingly removed from the workplace (Robinson, 1979:421; see also Bryner, 1981:126– 7). And as group after group has been added to the protected list the battle has increasingly become one not of groups against employers but of groups against groups for the same employment opportunities.

The points made by Robinson and Bryner are perhaps best illustrated by the thirteen years it took the bureaucracy and the courts to reach a decision when the Equal Employment Opportunity Commission (EEOC) charged the giant American retailer Sears, Roebuck & Company with discrimination in its employment practices on the basis of sex, national origin and race. The EEOC tried conciliation from 1973 to 1979 and when that failed took Sears to court. Sears retaliated by filing the suit against ten federal agencies referred to above. After that case was dismissed the EEOC filed five separate suits against Sears: four separate suits alleging discrimination in hiring against Blacks and Hispanics in specific Sears operations and a nationwide sex discrimination suit. Settlement was eventually reached on the four race discrimination cases but it was 1984 before the sex discrimination case actually went to trial. A final decision, absolving Sears of discriminating against women, was not reached until February 1986. The case is notable not only for the length of time it took to be resolved, but also for the $US20 million Sears was prepared to spend to win it (costs were awarded against the EEOC, that is, the public purse), and for the rather public brawl that ensued when each side brought in a 'feminist historian' to give expert testimony, a brawl which rebounded onto the American Historical Association and feminist scholars across America. It is also notable that a challenge was made and won to the sufficiency of statistical evidence alone (see Milkman, 1986; Cooper, 1986; Kessler-Harris, 1987; Riger, 1988).

US Congressional abdication of its legislative reponsibilities has, as Bryner points out, left the matter in the hands of the bureaucratic enforcement agencies and the courts. These two have tended to pull in opposite directions. Ironically, the approach adopted by the bureaucracy has led to superficiality while that of the most conservative arm of the American system of government, the judiciary, has from time to time aimed at the core of the radical potential that equal employment opportunity once had.

The approach of the bureaucracy

One of the most striking features of the fragmented and contradictory evaluations of American efforts to achieve equal employment opportunity is that they are almost exclusively quantitative (see, for example, Bocher, 1982; Cavalier and Slaughter, 1982; Clynch and Gaudin, 1982; Hitt and Keats, 1984; Stewart and Bullock, 1981); a series of studies of changes in numbers — numbers of minority group members and women going in, going up and, increasingly, going out again. What is largely unexamined are the changes (if any) to core values, criteria and practices which produce those changes in numbers, that is, any analysis of qualitative change.

Milward and Swanson argue that the response of an individual organisation to externally imposed demands for affirmative action compliance is likely to be one which seeks to minimise the uncertainty contained therein by complying with the demands to hire more minorities and women but at the same time 'minimizing the effects of change on the organisation by employing minority and female employees in organizational subunits which are isolated from the core activities of the organization' (1979:124). In effect employing them in the 'elephant burial grounds' of the organisation.

Affirmative Action Programs have been handled in such a way as to isolate and protect the entire core of employment relations, the core questions about the nature of work, from scrutiny. The result has been Equal Employment Opportunity (compliance) without equal employment opportunity (fundamental change). The programs are called 'results oriented' and as far as the agencies are concerned this means changes in numbers. Fed by time and resource constraints the production of numbers has become a self-perpetuating exercise in bureaucratic goal displacement which has ensured that the programs remain largely external to the organisations on which they have been imposed. The agencies demand, as the centrepiece of any affirmative action plan, a utilisation analysis of employees with reference to the protected groups. If any group is underutilised by comparison with statistics on availability (differently determined for different groups), they are required to demonstrate how and when that situation will be rectified. One of the complaints of Sears, Roebuck was that the government did not provide 'adequate statistical data with which private employment figures could be compared' (Bryner, 1981:411). An Ad Hoc Committee on Affirmative Action Statistics of the American Statistical Association in 1982 detailed some of the problems in this area:

- The possibility of double counting;
- The difficulty of trying to match ethnic identification based on self-identification (Census data) with that based on someone else's identification (employers);
- The non-availability of statistical data which would enable employers to meet the federal requirements that employers hire in accordance with 'the availability of people capable of performing the work, *or who might be trained to do so*' (Jaffe *et al*, 1982:321–332);
- The imprecise relationship between occupational categories required by enforcement agencies and occupational statistics provided by the Census;
- The smallness of some numerical goals for particular occupational categories for individual organisations, which are more appropriately regarded as case studies than statistical analyses.

Such numerical emphasis has undoubtedly been the cause of what *Time* magazine has called the 'bureaucratic idiocies [which] have marred the Government's attempts to end discrimination in employment', citing as an example the requirement that 'employers attempt to make sure that exactly 6.9 per cent of workers on Government financed construction jobs, including carpenters, laborers, and cement finishers be women' (Church, 1981).

More importantly, the pressure to produce numbers has meant that there has been little time and less incentive to analyse the causes of the numbers, the qualitative information on structural barriers and the value systems inherent in the employment criteria that produce the numbers. This has not gone unnoticed even if it remains to be rectified. In a study on naval shipyards, for example, Clynch and

Gaudin observe that among the sins of omission in Civil Service Guidelines on affirmative action procedures was a failure to request identification of practices having a discriminatory effect and investigation of the causes of underutilisation of minorities and women (1982:118).

In higher education, where more work has been done on the effects of the programs, the picture is even clearer: 'Its [AA/EEO office] major efforts are spent in gathering statistics for state and federal agencies rather than in educating a faculty badly in need of it' (Cavalier and Slaughter, 1982:389). The effect of this is that 'affirmative action is concerned primarily with who plays the game, and rather less with how the game is played' (Exum, 1983:394).

The real tragedy is the bureaucratic betrayal of the ideal that spawned the effort, an ideal which was interested in more than a simple change in the sex, race, colour or national origin of those at the top of organisational hierarchies. Writing as early as 1975 on dashed hopes for affirmative action in higher education, Gittell lamented that it had become a 'limited response to a series of individual complaints' and that the broader concept of institutional change had been lost, so that 'affirmative action in the University [is] no more than an illusion' (1975:43).

The Reagan years did nothing to shore up anybody's faith in government commitment to formal legislative affirmative action programs. A National Self-Monitoring Reporting System was introduced in 1984 to reduce the need to file reports with agencies; agencies were provided with ever dwindling resources to implement the programs and monitor their progress; and shifts in emphasis in implementation were guaranteed by shifts in the personnel heading the monitoring agencies.

The approach of the judiciary

In marked contrast to the approach of the American bureaucracy to equal employment opportunity, an approach which is so superficial that it barely manages to tap into work-based causes of inequality of employment opportunity, is that of the US Supreme Court. In some of its post-1970 sex discrimination decisions, the Court has moved directly into the world beyond work, to the allegedly separate 'private' world of family structure which is part and parcel of the network of causal factors making up the pattern of sex inequality. In an article highly critical of this action, Morton argues that since 1971 the Court has impugned the legitimacy of the traditional family structure in which women are socially and economically dependent (1984:475–477).

It is true that what the Court's decisions appear to have done is to begin to treat women as a class of individuals with rights rather than as people whose rights derive only from their relations to fathers (as daughters), to husbands (as wives) and to children (as mothers). The US Supreme Court is unlikely to continue in this almost inadvertently radical direction for much longer. Reagan changed the way the bureaucracy implements AA programs by changing the personnel at the top. His appointments to the Supreme Court, as well as Bush's, are expected to produce similar changes in direction in the Court's rulings. Already the Court has struck down the Richmond City set-aside (retrenchment) program. In a dissenting report Justice Thurgood Marshall described the majority decision as 'a deliberate and giant step backward in this Court's affirmative action jurisprudence' (*Off Our Backs*, 1989:4).

Australian beginnings

In the early days of Women's Liberation in Australia, as elsewhere, there was not much talk of equality. Obviously, some of the more concrete demands of the Movement embodied the concept of equality: equal pay for equal work or work of equal value, equal access to all forms of education, equal access to all forms of employment, equal right under the law and so on. These were important reforms, as was abortion law reform/repeal, which were to be fought for not only, or even most importantly, as ends in themselves but because women had to live and work in the here and now, struggling toward something called liberation — an altogether much broader, longer-term and far less easily definable goal. But in the arrogance of its early ignorance about prior outbursts of feminist rebellion, the Movement defined itself by what it thought its predecessors were and it was not: they were emancipationists, they wanted equality; the new Movement was liberationist and wanted something more radical (see Phillips, 1987: Ch 1). Indeed, the word feminist was rarely used among Women's Liberationists until the mid-1970s — unless the intention was to insult somebody by implying that they were 'merely reformist'. The problem with equality was that it implied 'equality with' — with whom? To do what? The process of internal debate within Women's Liberation Movements both here and overseas produced detailed critiques of patriarchal society. Critics of the aspiration of 'equality with men' held up the example of men in male dominated societies and asked, 'Is this what we really want?'

Perhaps the biggest problem the Movement had in trying to explain itself was to meet the demand for some vision of what the world and the people on it would look like in a liberated future. If the Movement was planning to tear down what was here and now, what did it intend to put in its place? To answer, as Virginia Woolf did in 1938, that 'if we have no example of what we wish to be we have, what is perhaps equally valuable, a daily and illuminating example of what we do not wish to be' was bad enough. To argue further that not only do we not know but that we cannot know because our unliberated minds cannot conceive adequately of such a future is intolerable.

Unable to legislate for liberation (a contradiction in terms anyway), mildly reformist governments tried legislating for equality — which is what some parts of the wider women's movement wanted all the time. This, in 1976, was what the newly elected Labor Government of New South Wales began to do with the introduction of its Anti-Discrimination Bill. Originally seeking to protect more disadvantaged groups than the then undemocratically appointed and conservative dominated New South Wales Legislative Council would accept, the Bill was amended and passed. Since 1977 it has been further amended to bring back in almost all of the groups and grounds initially proposed. In essence, the legislation acknowledges that there is a certain group of people who occupy most of the positions of power in society, who have access to and control over most of its resources, who determine the rules for allocating those resources and who, in the past, have been able to maintain their positions of power by means which are no longer considered 'fair'. If we turn the provisions of the New South Wales Anti-Discrimination Act around, what it says is that in the provision of goods and services, access to registered clubs, accommodation, education, access to public places and vehicles and employment, all people are now to be treated as if they were physically able, intellectually unimpaired, white, Anglo-Celtic, heterosexual males — that is, provided they can 'pass'.

The Anti-Discrimination Board handles complaints of discrimination by conciliation and, when that fails, by referring them to the Equal Opportunity Tribunal. The Tribunal was created in 1981 to overcome the difficulties the Board was facing in trying to fulfil two functions: firstly, that of research and community education opposing discriminatory practices and secondly, that of an impartial quasi-judicial body hearing cases where discrimination had been alleged.

The Tribunal has the power to award damages and began to do so in 1984, eight years after the Act came into force. As far as the Board was concerned eight years was long enough for employers, public and private, to familiarise themselves with those of their practices that were unlawful and those that were not. By American standards the damages awarded are peanuts: $A34 872 in a case of sexist harassment, $A31 891 in a case of sex discrimination in retirement provisions and most recently (1989) $A40 000 (the maximum damages the Tribunal can award) in several cases of unequal treatment of women flight attendants in promotion opportunities.

3

Bureaucrats

Being a discussion of some of the dilemmas EEO poses for bureaucracy at the theoretical level, an account of the bureaucratic processes that have been established to implement EEO legislation at state and Commonwealth levels and an analysis of the problems the new 'managerialism' has created for EEO.

The relationship between equal employment and bureaucracy at a theoretical level is as complex and problematical as that between EEO programs and actual bureaucracies (private and public) in the real world of politics.

Theoretical dilemmas

Weber, patron saint of modern bureaucracy, characterised bureaucracy, as hierarchically organised with delegation of authority and specialisation, functioning according to rational principles and in an impersonal manner. Actual bureaucracies, in both public and private sectors, approximate more or less to the ideal or pure theoretical form. Changing social attitudes certainly generate contradictions challenging that ideal type or making its achievement more difficult. EEO, subscribing in principle to the ideal type but itself born of changing social attitudes and seeking to reflect them, may be caught in these contradictions. Take, for instance, calls for a representative bureaucracy. There are two parts to the argument mounted in support of a representative bureaucracy. Both claim the desirability of bureaucracies 'representative' of the public they serve while leaving unclear how representativeness is to be gauged. The first is based on a value judgement — the members of 'the public, because they pay the taxes which finance the provision of public services, ought to have an equal opportunity to attain the jobs created to deliver those public services. Those jobs should not be reserved for special sections of the public (Eisenstein, 1985:73). This is the weaker of the two arguments because it leaves unanswered questions like the position of people who cannot pay taxes because they cannot get a job and whether those who pay more taxes ought therefore to be given first crack at public service jobs. The latter would probably result in public services looking much like the ones we already have. The second argument for representative bureaucracy is more utilitarian and more telling. If the role of the public services is to serve the public, to devise and implement public policies and deliver services, unless all sections of the public are somehow represented in those processes the resultant policies are likely to be deficient and the delivery of public service inefficient. The history of Australian social welfare is littered with examples of policies which could not be implemented because they were designed by the wrong people, some with the best of intentions. Consultation is one way to overcome that deficiency but the participation of the intended beneficiaries in the process of policy development and service delivery is likely to be more effective. Real world public services have tacitly acknowledged the validity of this argument in support of a more representative bureaucracy by involving particular communities in some aspects of the policy process: for example, the employment of liaison officers to assist public services in their relationships with particular Aboriginal and ethnic communities, the establishment of units or bureaux specifically concerned with issues of importance to women, and the involvement of the gay community in the development of educational programs aimed at stopping the spread of AIDS through that community. If public services were more representative than they currently are, the argument goes, all of these specific skills would be fully integrated into them and there would be no need for the creation of special positions or units. In addition, approaching majority culture problems from minority perspectives could be creative. Yet there is some question of how arguments for a representative bureaucracy fit with its projection in an ideal form.

There is also the long list of pathologies to which bureaucracies are susceptible and which give the originally neutral and descriptive term its pejorative overtones. Most of these are almost the logical conclusions to Weber's original criteria for the functioning of the bureaucratic staff. With promotion based on seniority or merit and awarded according to the judgement of superiors, Robert Michels, writing in 1915, saw inevitable (and undesirable) consequences:

> Bureaucracy is the sworn enemy of individual liberty, and of all bold initiative in matters of internal policy. The dependence upon superior authorities characteristic of the average employer suppresses individuality and gives to the society in which employees predominate a narrow petty-bourgeois and philistine stamp. The bureaucratic spirit corrupts character and engenders moral poverty. In every bureaucracy we may observe place-hunting, a mania for promotion, and obsequiousness towards

those on whom promotion depends; there is arrogance towards inferiors and servility towards superiors. (Michels, 1962:191)

Writing later, and in less colourful language, Robert Merton identified several other pathologies which resulted from conflicts built in to bureaucratic structure and functioning. Inflexibility, or Veblen's 'trained incapacity', is inherent in bureaucracies — 'actions based upon training and skills which have been successfully applied in the past may result in inappropriate responses *under changed conditions'* (Merton, 1952: 364). Goal displacement can also be expected when adherence to rules becomes an end in itself, so familiar in the phenomenon of red tape (Merton, 1952:365—366). One *Yes Minister* episode had central administrators frothing because a local authority had not completed its statutory return of statistical information and filed it with the Department:

> This was a definition of evil? Someone who doesn't return his blue form? 'Yes', I said with heavy irony, 'I don't see how life still goes on in South Derbyshire.'
> Sir Humphrey took my remark at face value. 'Exactly, Minister. They really are in a class of their own for incompetence.' (Lynn and Jay, 1988: 484)

Merton also saw that the way bureaucracies were structured, and the internal demands made upon officials, lead almost inevitably to the less appealing aspects of bureaucratic personality, resistance to change and the haughtiness and arrogance of the bureaucrat when dealing with the public (1952, 367—370). The capacity of bureaucracies to absorb, transform and render harmless (to themselves) ideas foreign to their ethos, a capacity Selznick referred to as 'coöptation' (1952:35), is similarly built in to the ideal. It provides bureaucracies with stability and consistency over time, the desirable side of the coin, but it does not augur well, even at this theoretical level, for ideas about reforming the bureaucracy in the direction of increased representativeness. We can expect EEO programs to be either resisted or rendered harmless or both and we can expect genuine eeo to be almost a pipedream.

If EEO programs are aimed solely at changing the sex or race of the occupants of bureaucratic staff positions then theoretically, provided these new occupants are prepared to subscribe to traditional bureaucratic values, norms and expectations, in short, to be assimilated into that organisational culture, such programs should be able to overcome the initial resistance to their introduction. But they will work only, or primarily, to the benefit of those who can become assimilated, who can adopt, or at least adapt to, the dominant values and patterns of work. On the other hand, equal employment opportunity which requires the bureaucratic culture, rather than aspiring personnel, to change is facing an altogether different form and degree of resistance. Weber made no comment on the sex of bureaucrats; he did not need to, unquestionably they were men. On top of that, the defining characteristics of his rational bureaucratic system (hierarchy, divisions, separations, competition, discipline and control) are precisely those associated with masculinity.

While EEO programs may be perceived by individual men as threatening to their masculinity, genuine equal employment opportunity, which requires changes to the nature of bureaucracies, threatens the dominance of masculinity as the organising principle of bureaucracies. As Franzway, Court and Connell note, 'The rise of bureaucratic forms of organisation is historically linked to the rise of new forms of hegemonic masculinity oriented to technical knowledge and personal competitiveness displacing aristocratic models of masculinity' (1989: 46). Individuals who move into staff positions may be successfully socialised and treated as one of the boys, or they may resist socialisation and be seen as trouble makers, unwilling to adapt or just plain difficult. Similarly, the EEO programs themselves are likely either to be absorbed and rendered harmless, that is, bureaucratised, or if they are seen as more threatening, to be marginalised and rendered harmless by being made vulnerable to pruning or decease by benign neglect.

Practical dilemmas

Quite early in the development of the second wave of Australian feminism, some women made the difficult but conscious decision to seek to influence public policy by entering the public services. The other major option for exercising influence was through the political party system. From time to time there have been fantasies about the idea of forming a feminist political party which would attract the electoral support of a majority of women at the polls, but it had never moved much beyond fantasy. It is the road the greenies have followed quite successfully. Some women's movement activists were members of existing political parties whose chances of constituting the balance of power in parliament, let alone forming a government, were only marginally greater than those of a feminist party. Those feminists who were also members of the Australian Labor Party (ALP) battled at every level for that inch of ground which would put women's issues on the agenda for party debate. Complex and at times corrupt procedures meant that very few women had a chance of being preselected for even marginal seats and no way of winning preselection in safe

ALP seats. The 1972 Women's Electoral Lobby exercise of publicising
the views of candidates on selected women's issues was a tacit
acknowledgment of the inability of women to influence the major
parties from within.

Decisions to enter the public services were difficult for obvious
reasons. The state has not been merely unresponsive to the needs of
women for most of its history but has itself been an instrument in
their continued subordination. It has denied women the right to
control their own fertility, it has enshrined the unequal pay of women
workers, it has restricted the entry of women into particular areas of
employment. The state has also refused properly to enforce laws it has
enacted: laws against rape and domestic violence against women are
obvious examples. The role of the state in the oppression of Aboriginal
people is even more stark because more brutal. Through its determination of priorities and allocation of resources, it allows disease and
other factors to kill twice as many Aboriginal as non-Aboriginal
children (Gray, 1988). Given this history, was it not totally unrealistic
to expect to be able to produce what amounted to a huge shift in the
role of the state by entering it? Yet it was precisely the degree of state
involvement (and the selective lack of involvement) in everyday life
that made it essential to try. And it was easier for women to obtain
jobs in the public service than to be elected as part of government. It
was also less distasteful since it did not demand the wheeling and
dealing and unpalatable compromises associated with party politics.
Or so it seemed at the time. Moreover, there was an appreciation of
the scope that public servants have for widening or narrowing policy
options and the role that implementation of policy can play in its
success or demise.

The difficulties of following this path became obvious with (and for)
the first appointments by governments of women's advisors in the
mid-1970s (see Franzway, Court and Connell; 1989:138). Who or
what they were supposed to represent and how, and what their
appointments signified, were contentious issues within the women's
movement. More difficult was the question of whether or not to seek
and accept government funds for women's movement initiatives such
as health centres, rape crisis centres and women's refuges. Government
funds do not come without strings attached. The conflicts for the individual women who entered the public services, the femocrats as they
have become known, were and are legion. They revolve in the main
around the question of how to avoid the trap of individual goal
displacement, that is, becoming so caught up in the rituals and
politics of influencing policy that you forget why you wanted to. (See
on this the growing body of analysis: Lynch, 1984; Franzway, 1986;
Franzway, Court and Connell, 1989; Yeatman, 1990.)

The broad push for equal employment opportunity was an example of this general mobilisation of the women's movement to engagement with the state. Indeed, one of the earliest demonstrations of Sydney Women's Liberation, in August 1970, was in protest at the New South Wales Public Service Board's practice of advertising vacancies in separate Men's and Women's columns of the *Sydney Morning Herald*.

But there was (and is) a huge gap between the kind of equal employment opportunity the women's movement, particularly the women's liberation part of the movement, wanted and the Equal Employment Opportunity (EEO) Programs that emerged in the late 1970s. In fact, the first piece of Australian EEO legislation did not come directly out of the women's movement. It came out of the climate for reform that the sexual liberation movements had created but it was fathered by Peter Wilenski's *Review of New South Wales Government Administration* (1977). The *Review* dealt with all aspects of government administration in New South Wales — policy development, budgeting processes, regionalisation, staffing and administration, effectiveness, efficiency and coordination, organisational change, worker participation, service delivery, freedom of information as well as equal employment opportunity. In this respect it was part of a long tradition of enquiries into public services in Australia (Smith and Weller, 1978). Using the language of both efficiency and social justice, the *Review* identified, named and proposed remedies for a long list of bureaucratic pathologies.

The proposed remedy for unequal employment opportunity in the New South Wales public service was inherently problematical. The employment policies and practices of the bureaucracy were to be reformed by the creation of a new and separate arm of that bureaucracy. This provided the opponents of the legislation with a seemingly not unreasonable objection. It was not that they were against equal opportunity in employment — what they were against was 'the establishment of a new bureaucratic arm of government [which] is akin to using a sledgehammer to crack a walnut' NSW Parliamentary Debates, Hansard Vol CLIII, 19. March 1980:6143–6145).

By the time the Commonwealth Affirmative Action legislation was debated in 1986 the political climate had changed considerably: deregulation and small government had become much more appealing slogans. Even so, increased government regulation of the private sector required the expenditure of government funds on a new bureaucracy. Debates in the Parliament were bitter on the inevitable expansion of the new bureaucratic office when other government expenditure was being cut. (See Commonwealth of Australia Parliamentary Debates, Senate, Vol 5.116:125–134, 176–184.)

What is required by the legislation

Different pieces of EEO legislation enacted in Australia may be dissimilar in the groups they cover, yet in their language and their requirements of organisations they are very close. Language is particularly interesting in the light of the shifts in ethos that are being introduced into Australian public services whereby 'public administration' is being transformed into 'the management of the public sector'. EEO legislative requirements in New South Wales look almost like a pilot program for the new managerialism which is taking over Australian public services and ironically endangering EEO programs themselves. The discussion following focuses on legislation in New South Wales (the state which pioneered the legislation in Australia) and at the Commonwealth level.

New South Wales

The legislation which embodied Wilenski's EEO reform proposals took the form of an amendment to the New South Wales Anti-Discrimination Act (1977) — the addition of Part IXA which was to apply to New South Wales government departments and statutory authorities and to cover women and members of racial minorities. Introduced in 1980, the amendment set out the requirements of the Part, created the Office of the Director of Equal Opportunity in Public Employment (ODEOPE) which was located within the Premier's Department, and detailed the penalty for non-compliance with the legislation. Each organisation covered by the legislation is charged with preparing and implementing an Equal Employment Opportunity Management Plan and with lodging a copy of the Plan with the ODEOPE 'as soon as practicable' after it has been prepared. The initial deadline gave organisations one year.

> **122J** (2) The management plan of an authority shall include provisions relating to
> (a) the devising of policies and programmes by which the objects of this Part are to be achieved;
> (b) the communication of those policies and programmes to persons within the authority;
> (c) the collection and recording of appropriate information;
> (d) the review of personnel practices within the authority (including recruitment techniques, selection criteria, training and staff development programmes, promotion and transfer policies and pattern, and conditions of service) with a view to the identification of any discriminatory practices);
> (e) the setting of goals or targets, where these may be reasonably determined, against which the success of the

management plan in achieving the objects of this Part may be assessed;

(f) the means, other than those referred to in paragraph (e), of evaluating the policies and programmes referred to in paragraph (a);

(g) the revision and amendment of the management plan; and

(h) the appointment of persons within the authority to implement the provisions referred to in paragraphs (a)−(g).

Section 122M states that:

Where the Director is dis-satisfied with any matter relating to the preparation or implementation of a management plan by an authority or any failure or omission of an authority with respect to the preparation or implementation of a management plan, the Director may refer the matter to the [Anti-Discrimination] Board.

The Anti-Discrimination Board may hold an investigation into the reference and at the conclusion of any such investigation may make recommendations to the Director or the authority and/or report to the Minister on the matter.

While there was some support within the public sector for the implementation of EEO as spelt out in the legislation, some agencies were indifferent and others directly hostile. There was, for example, a difference between the responses of departments and those of authorities, the latter being generally less tractable. No doubt this was tied to the fact that while departments were covered by the Public Service Act and had no room for movement, authorities have their own acts of parliament with which they are required to comply. After three years most departments and authorities had lodged their management plans with the Director of Equal Opportunity in Public Employment but 16 of the 77 had not lodged a satisfactory plan, in three cases had not submitted a plan at all. Yet in 1985 one of the authorities which lodged an early, and it is said exemplary, management plan was involved in a sexual harassment case brought before the Equal Opportunity Tribunal. The Tribunal found for the complainant, and reports of the case suggest a workplace in which sexism remained rampant (see, for example, Ferguson, 1985:9).

In December 1983 universities and colleges of advanced education in New South Wales were scheduled under Part IXA of that state's Anti-Discrimination Act. The history of the scheduling was relatively short but by no means smooth for unlike government departments these institutions of higher education have a measure of autonomy in their systems of governance, an autonomy which they cherish and which presents something of a dilemma to state politicians. Nonetheless, as Thornton (1984:19) points out, while these institutions are variously covered by their own Acts of Incorporation they are 'public institutions, established by public Acts and supported by public funds'. They are therefore subject to public laws regarding both education and employment.

Certainly a number of campus-based women's groups were agitating to have the higher education sector covered by affirmative action legislation, although even in the autumn of 1983 the government's preference was for the introduction of self-administered equal employment programs by that sector. But attitudes changed — although not those of the governing bodies of colleges of advanced education and universities — and in December of that same year these institutions were scheduled under the same legislation (state) as government authorities. In mid-1984 the physically disabled were added to the list of disadvantaged groups to receive the benefits of the EEO programs.

While it was politically well located in the Premier's Department, the Office of the Director, like its American counterparts, was given totaly inadequate resources to fulfil its obligations. Since it was both to advise and assist organisations to comply with the legislation, and to determine whether they had done so, there was some conflict of interest. The Office of the Director dealt with this difficulty in two ways. The first was to insist on uniformity of approach, both from organisations covered by the legislation and to the disparate groups who were its intended beneficiaries. That the 100 or so public sector organisations covered include the huge, geographically dispersed and occupationally-diverse State Rail Authority, which in 1986 employed 41 269 people, the Meat Industry Authority with 17 employees (Public Service Board of New South Wales:1986) and all New South Wales universities and colleges of advanced education, was not (could not be) weighted as a variable. Despite different statutory bases, sources of funds and organisational cultures each was to prepare the Equal Employment Opportunity Management Plan referred to in the legislation according to strict guidelines issued by the Office of the Director. The format was standard and gave major emphasis to objectives and strategies: broad objectives, specific actions, corrective strategies, innovative strategies, general measures, creative measures, responsibility, target date and evaluation procedures (Ziller, 1980:52—59). Similarly a uniform approach to the very different groups covered by the legislation was required, leading to some thoughtlessly worded suggestions. Since, for example, assertiveness training appeared to have been of benefit to some women it was advocated for the physically disabled to enable them to 'stand up for themselves'. Organisations which were able to recruit tertiary educated women were castigated for not trying hard enough to recruit tertiary educated Aboriginal people, ignoring the disparity in numbers of each group going on to tertiary education. (See, for example, *Annual Report of Office of the Director of Equal Opportunity in Public Employment*, 1986:6, 18.) The overriding emphasis was on numbers: 'In the end, the success or failure of affirmative action depends on statistical results. *An affirmative action plan is successful only if it results in a more equitable distribution of women and migrants in personnel statistics*' (1986).

Anyone who has ever had to assess the performance of students by examination will acknowledge that it is quicker to mark 100 multiple choice questionnaire answer forms (even machines can do that) than 100 essays. Which gives a better indication of how much students have learned is much more debatable. The emphasis on numbers, on statistical results, is enormously problematic.

The second way the Office of the Director sought to deal with the inadequate resources allocated to it was completely in harmony with the insistence on uniformity. This was to cloak EEO in the mantle of the new managerialism, with its emphasis on 'calculable outcomes', allowing EEO in turn to introduce the new managerialism (wearing the cloak of equity, access and participation) into the public service. But as Yeatman points out, the two do not sit together comfortably, they have different political agendas, are premised on different interests and attract opposed constituencies (1990:6-7).

EEO was made a management issue from the start, with responsibilities filtering from the top down to all levels. Neither the legislation nor the guidelines required consultation, either with trade unions or with those the legislation is supposed to benefit. The latter became target groups, that is, on the receiving end of what management determined would be of benefit to them. The New South Wales Program ran into difficulties with the New South Wales Trades and Labor Council very early on over guidelines for handling grievances. The draft guidelines from ODEOPE not only neglected to acknowledge the role that trade unions have traditionally played in the resolution of grievances, they made no mention whatsoever of the existence of unions. And by making the intended beneficiaries the targets of programs (objects rather than subjects) established or endorsed by management, the benefits they are to receive are those considered to have value by and to management. They include assertiveness training courses, how-to-supervise courses, training to ensure career advancement. While no one would deny that individuals should be able to develop their skills and abilities, use them constructively and be rewarded accordingly, the emphasis on getting target groups out of the jobs they are in and into the jobs occupied by dominant culture members is worrying. It reinforces the low value placed on those jobs; leaves unexamined (and undervalued) the skills required to perform those jobs; leaves unanswered the question of who will perform them; ignores (and leaves unchallenged) the hierarchical shape of most bureaucracies (that is, not everyone can reach the top); excludes from debate a whole range of options for organising differently the work that has to be done; and may not be what the intended beneficiaries of the legislation actually think would be of most benefit to them.

Commonwealth Public Service

The Commonwealth Government's earliest move into the area of affirmative action dates back to the First World War in a program which went far beyond the limits of what would be regarded as acceptable today for women or any other group covered by equal employment opportunity legislation. It was a program of absolute preference in Commonwealth employment for soldiers returned from the war. Between 1918 and 1932, of the 1779 appointments to junior and clerical administrative positions, only 3 per cent went to non-returned soldiers (Crisp, 1978:438). Bean, Australia's official historian of the war, commented that

> under the particular form of preference for returned soilders
> between the wars, recruits for most of the Service had for half a
> generation been exclusively old soldiers — a procedure that not
> infrequently turned first-class tradesmen into second-class clerks.
> (Bean, 1943:71—72)

The Australian Public Service, as a significant employer of labour in its own right, as well as a barometer of changing employment mores, has an interesting history of changing criteria of eligibility for appointment to the Service:
- Between 1915 and 1949 women were barred from competing for appointment to the clerical division of the Service;
- 1933 saw legislation enacted which permitted graduate recruitment, but to no more than 10 per cent of the positions in the Service;
- 1960 saw seniority removed as the criterion for promotion within the Service and the abolition of preference for ex-servicemen;
- Eligibility for employment in the Service was extended to the handicapped in 1962, to married women in 1966, and to diabetics in 1967 so that by 1970 over 8000 people, previously ineligible, were employed in the Service (Thompson, 1986:43—46).

The gradual evening out of formal criteria of eligibility for appointment was part and parcel of the seemingly never-ending stream of the attempts to improve the Service. It was a precursor to more active steps (never quite as proactive as those taken to assist returned soldiers) toward the formal introduction of Equal Employment Opportunity Programs in the 1970s.

In 1975 the Public Service Board (the regulator for employment in the Australian Public Service established an EEO Section to develop and implement EEO policies and programs. In 1978 the Section was upgraded to a branch and renamed the EEO Bureau (Radford, 1985:54). Groups covered by the program were women, Aborigines, people with a physical disability and migrants. The EEO Bureau's job was to provide a consulting service on the preparation of EEO programs by departments which were to report back to the Public Service Board on their progress (Public Service Board, 1984:6). But in May 1984, the Policy Discussion Paper on Affirmative Action issued by the Department of Prime Minister and Cabinet was less than sanguine on the success of these measures. The uneven performance and level of failure was not simply because objectives were not met but because objectives were not set. According to the Discussion Paper, the reason lay in the fact that all action was voluntary. That is, lacking any formal requirement that the policies be adopted and programs implemented, and lacking negative sanctions in the event of dereliction, departments demonstrated varying degrees of commitment. Some took active steps towards implementation, others did little or nothing. EEO functions were given scant time and EEO staff low status (Department of Prime Minister and Cabinet, 1984:36—37). It was the same with statutory authorities.

The Public Service Reform Act of 1984 made discrimination on a range of grounds (including sexual preference) unlawful in Commonwealth employment. The Act also made the preparation and implementation of EEO programs by all Australian Public Service departments a legal requirement. Groups covered by the Act are Aboriginal and Torres Strait Island people, migrants whose first language is not English, women, people who are physically or mentally disabled and 'any other class of persons declared by the regulations to be a designated group' (Radford, 1985:64). The EEO programs that are to be prepared are defined as having six steps: examining employment practices to identify discriminatory practices; disseminating information about the program; consultation with unions; collecting and recording information; assessing the effectiveness of the program and following the guidelines issued by the EEO Bureau of the Australian Public Service Board (Ronalds, 1987b:87). In 1986 new regulations extended coverage of the Act to some Commonwealth statutory authorities and other government organisations such as the Australian

Security Intelligence Organisation (ASIO), the Australian Broadcasting Corporation, Australia Post, Telecom and the Australian
Federal Police.

No sooner had work begun on department and authority EEO
programs than yet another review of the Australian Public Service
recommended sweeping reforms moving the Service even further into
a managerialist culture. The Public Service Board was abolished and
responsibility for EEO was devolved to departments which would
include an EEO section in their annual reports only. A small monitoring unit was to be retained in the Public Service Commission (the
successor to the Public Service Board) (Sawer, 1987:95). The resultant
downgrading of EEO in the Australian Public Service was not the
purpose of the reform; EEO became an innocent bystander knocked
down by public sector reformers in their headlong rush to emulate the
private sector by adopting the latter's management techniques and
forms or organisation. For EEO in the public sector, the difficulties
arise not only from downgrading specific EEO programs but also
from upping the stakes for entry into the upper echelons of the service
by adoption of the management values of the private sector—the
fetishism of technique, orientation to results and teleological pro-
miscuity (Yeatman, 1990:14—36). Many in Australia's public services
might well identify with Petronius:

> We trained hard...but it seemed that every time we were
> beginning to form up into teams we would be reorganised ...I
> was to learn later in life that we tend to meet any new situation by
> reorganising; and a wonderful method it can be for creating the
> illusion of progress while producing confusion, inefficiency, and
> demoralization.

Commonwealth Affirmative Action Legislation

Early in 1984, and after a stormy passage, the Commonwealth passed
the Sex Discrimination Act. Through this legislation Australia took
steps in response to its obligations as a signatory to the United
Nations Convention on the Elimination of All Forms of Discrimination
Against Women. Essentially complaints-based, it identifies as grounds
for complaint discriminatory treatment in employment and various
conditions of employment on the basis of sex, marital status—including de facto relationships—pregnancy and discrimination involving
sexual harassment. The Racial Discrimination Act, again complaints-
based, had already been enacted by the Commonwealth Parliament in
1975. Enactment of this legislation followed Australia's ratification of
the United Nations International Convention on the Elimination of
All Forms of Racial Discrimination. In this case, the grounds for

complaint in employment and various conditions of employment lie in discrimination against people on the basis of their race, colour, descent and national or ethnic origins. Since 1981, the Human Rights Commission has provided the machinery to deal with such complaints. There is no provision in either of these pieces of legislation for affirmative action.

Originally, in a private member's bill on sex discrimination introduced in 1981 by Senator Susan Ryan, affirmative action had been tied to anti-discrimination. This overture was, however, unsuccessful. Since the notion of affirmative action is much more problematical and generates more resistance, it was seen as prudent to separate the two prongs of policy in order to secure enactment of the anti-discrimination provisions. Even so, the carriage of the legislation was beset by real political difficulties. Lobby groups argued that the legislation was a direct attack on the family: it was alleged to devalue the role of wife and mother, mysteriously promote the neglect of children and attack the central position of the provident husband. The whole ideology of the family was claimed to be under seige. Given the strength of this ideology the political path was strewn with broken glass. If complaints-based legislation could generate such hostility it is not hard to imagine the responses of these same groups of people to affirmative action legislation.

Having secured the passage of the Sex Discrimination Act the Commonwealth Government produced the Policy Discussion Paper on Affirmative Action for Women. At the Commonwealth level the various forms of social disadvantage are seen by the government as requiring different forms of legislative, administrative and indeed broad social response. The ragbag approach has been eschewed. Apart from any steps taken to accord land rights to Aboriginal people, in itself a sorry tale, the question of legislating for affirmative action for other people tagged disadvantaged has been toyed with but not formally broached.

The Policy Discussion Paper on Affirmative Action for Women was directed to the private sector of Australian industry and commerce, although it was also seen to have application in the realm of higher education. In it the government expressed its commitment to 'encouraging policies which enable women who wish to enter the labour force the opportunity to participate fully in employment' (Department of Prime Minister and Cabinet, 1984:1). It was not a question of imposing requirements but it did bruit the possibility of legislation. At the same time as the Policy Discussion Paper was tabled in the Parliament, the government announced three affirmative action initiatives. A Working Party on Affirmative Action was established, an Affirmative Action Pilot Program was introduced and an Affirmative

Action Resource Unit was created to back up the Working Party and participants in the Pilot Program.

The Working Party invited submissions on the government's proposals for affirmative action for women. Groups or associations implacably opposed to legislation in this area held extremely conservative views on women's and men's traditional roles. Opposition was frequently given a religious flavour and certainly drew support from arguments of the New Right. Other opposition came from organisations in the business sector, including a number of participants in the pilot program. In broad terms they supported the concept of equal employment opportunity but were against legislation requiring prescribed affirmative action programs. Not all of these groups, however, were ill-disposed towards facilitative legislation which would enhance progress undertaken voluntarily by individual organisations. Apart from those women included in the opposition from the extreme right submissions, women's groups favoured legislation, although again views differed as to who should be covered.

The Pilot Program was set to run for a year. Its objectives included not only a demonstration of the painlessness and effectiveness of affirmative action, but also the identification and assessment of classes of difficulties for employers and employees which might surface. Organisations seeking to participate in the Pilot Program were required to have 100 or more employees; this was in recognition of the difficulties of formulating, and implementing, meaningful affirmative action programs in firms employing relatively few people. Eventually 28 companies from the private sector and three institutions of higher education were chosen as volunteers. They represented a distribution in scale, location and geographical spread, structure and culture.

At the end of the Pilot Program the Working Party submitted its final report. Guided by the experiences of the trial program and of the states where EEO Programs had been implemented long enough to identify weaknesses, legislation was drafted. Although there was some vitriolic debate on the Bill in the Senate there was, curiously, not the general mobilisation and outcry against the legislation that had attended the passage of the Sex Discrimination Act two years earlier. The legislation was passed and the Act proclaimed on 1 October 1986. The Affirmative Action Agency was established, its charge being to bring the legislation into effect. While there are strong similarities between this and other affirmative action legislation in operation in Australia, there are some significant differences, the most important of these being the requirements to consult with trade unions and to consult with employees, which clearly open the way for women to have some say in matters directly affecting them as members of staff. There is also a requirement that the legislation be reviewed as to its effectiveness in achieving its objectives. The Affirmative Action Agency had decided that it would review the legislation and its own role in implementing it at the end of five years of operation of the Act—in 1992. The announcement in August 1989 of a Parliamentary Committee of Inquiry on Equal Opportunity and Equal Status for Australian Women troubled the Agency, largely because it regards the exercise as premature.

The coverage of Commonwealth legislation left, curiously, a visible and incongruous hole. While government departments, the private sector and higher education institutions were required to introduce affirmative action programs, statutory authorities were not. In 1987 the Commonwealth Government introduced legislation to correct this bizarre state of affairs.

The 1987−88 *Annual Report* of the Affirmative Action Agency (1988) is the first to contain evaluations of the reports submitted to the Agency by all higher education institutions and 230 of those private sector employers (of 1000 or more people) required to make their first reports in that year. The 99 per cent response rate cited in the 1987− 88 *Report* indicates a high degree of compliance with the reporting requirements of the legislation. Yet to claim, as the *Report* does, that it 'indicates that affirmative action legislation is accepted by Australian employers' (Preface) is a rather optimistic assessment of what filing a report with the Agency signifies. Some private sector employers and some institutions of higher education who have been deemed to be making good progress have been awarded 'koala stamps'. Even so, the claims of the Minister to whom the Agency is responsible read as extravagant:

> We are a long way beyond the question of whether affirmative action is acceptable to employers. Almost all large companies are now participating. It just makes good commercial and management sense to use women in your organisations. The bottom line is does it make money; and the bottom line answer is yes. (*Financial Review*, 11 Nov. 1988)

Since the beginning of 1989 organisations with 100 employees or more have been brought under the legislation and the 1988−89 *Annual Report* takes a slightly more cautious view. The 97 per cent compliance rate is taken to indicate 'the serious regard employers have for the the legislation' (Preface). It is still too early to make any assessment of the impact of the legislation on employment opportunities for women. Crucial to that assessment, whether it is carried out by the Agency (which it should probably not be) or by independent researchers (which it probably should be), are:
• The clear delineation of criteria for determining first, how much (if

any) change in employment opportunities for women has occurred over a specified time period and second, how much of that change can legitimately be attributed to the legislation;

• Some way of actually matching reality as it is represented in organisation reports to the Agency and reality as it is experienced in the work place.

At the moment the Agency does not have the powers enjoyed by the Commissioner of Taxation to try to find out what kind of truth, or whose truth, is contained in those reports. It is cautionary to refer to submissions made to the House of Representatives Standing Committee on Legal and Constitutional Affairs Inquiry into Equal Opportunity and Equal Status for Australian Women. Some are commendatory of programs and legislation, a small number are condemnatory, most are qualified.

The Commonwealth legislation does contain several improvements on state legislative programs. In addition to the requirements for consultation with unions and women employees the Agency has adopted a more flexible approach to reporting. There is a recognition that the organisations covered by the legislation vary enormously in size, structures, organisational cultures and capacity to change quickly. Absent too is the pre-eminent position accorded to numbers in the New South Wales program.

Numbers bloody numbers

There is a clear logic to the requirement that numbers be produced to 'prove' non-discrimination since they were required to 'prove' discrimination. The truth is that numbers can prove neither. In the early 1970s, when large numbers of women in Australia (as elsewhere) began to articulate their resentment at discrimination based on sex, they used what at the time was their major source of evidence — their own experiences and those of other women. Such evidence was then — and is now — dismissed as 'subjective', 'unscientific', 'hearsay' and 'tales from the agony column' (Partington, 1984:127). Hard evidence was called for — numbers which were both 'objective' and 'scientific'. Feminist objections to the obsession with numbers were fundamental. They argued that such 'objectivity' was false and misleading and that human experience cannot be reduced to numbers for the sake of convenience and dismissed as irrelevant if it is not quantifiable. Nor were feminists alone in taking these views. But while not abandoning their stance in the methodological debates, feminists accepted that if action to redress past and continuing injustices was to be dependent on the production of numbers, then numbers would be produced. And they were, by the crateful. Disbelievers were to be fed the numbers they demanded until, with any luck, they would choke on them. Study after study, in country after country, reduced organisation after organisation to metres of computer printout which was rarely read.

Numbers can be a useful tool in analysis of data but they cannot take the place of analysis. Some of the most common problems with over reliance on numbers are as follows.

Numbers can tell you something about how many but they cannot tell you how

Where numbers can be of use is in aggregating large quantities of raw data so they they can be more easily manipulated. In a sense a translation is done on raw data but it is essential that once the manipulation has been completed the information is interpreted and presented in a meaningful form. As an example of the potential for confusion, an organisation may be required to report how many additional women, Aboriginal people and physically disabled employees it has put on over a one year period. Provided with separate boxes, it is possible to enter the number 1 into each box although the entries represented but one person — a physically disabled Aboriginal woman.

Correlations compiled in endless tables of cross-tabulations can be even more misleading. Of themselves they can show relationships between variables but give no information on causes, which in itself can be confusing. For example, a medical journal once reported what on the surface is a startling correlation — the larger the volume of blood a hospital patient receives in transfusion the more likely the patient is to die.

One EEO management plan submitted to ODEOPE was 8 centimetres thick. Of its 590 pages, six formed an introduction, 44 were devoted to a review of personnel practices, 85 to objectives and 455 to numbers.

Numbers can be misused to make apples feel really rotten about not being pears

The ODEOPE *Annual Report* for 1983 contains the following figures:

> . . . The following other departments and declared authorities have established identified positions for migrants:
> Public Service board: 185 positions
> Fish Marketing Board: 1 position (clerk/wheeler)
> Magistrates Courts Administration: 3 clerks of Petty Sessions
> Government Stores Department: 60 staff contact and Inspector positions

Housing Commission: 1 position (for person speaking Chinese language)...

The Public Service Board certainly looks good compared with the Fish Marketing Board or even the Government Stores Department, but is it? We need to be provided with a lot more contextual information to make any sense of the numbers. How many employees *in toto* does each area have? In what sectors of the labour force do they recruit? What are their functions? What changes (if any) do these numbers indicate and to what?

Numbers don't tell you why

How many employers put numbers in boxes simply to meet the demands of legislation or government policy? A department may put on six new women apprentices in carpentry. It records the fact with numbers but not why. Does it accept that good apprentices are good apprentices no matter their sex? Were employers conscious of someone breathing down their neck? Did the government subsidy that went with putting on women apprentices lead them to do so? Were there no male applicants? Does it matter? After all, six women apprentices were employed. What if the legislation were repealed? What if the subsidy disappeared? Why does make a difference, especially if you are looking to lasting change.

Numbers narrow the field of vision

By representing variations in numerical forms, the quantitative approach tends to direct our attention away from the evaluation of the concepts and variables themselves. (Young, 1979:63−69)

When numbers were produced to prove discrimination they came last, following on a huge outflow of qualitative evidence. They crowned a vast body of reasoning, argument and experiential data, not all of which was translatable into numbers but which was still available in messy non-numeric form. The numbers required by some as proof of non-discrimination seem to have been given the status of both necessary and sufficient evidence. But what of those practices which cannot be reduced to numbers without gross distortion?

If we want to know why more men than women are likely to be promoted within an organisation part of the answer may lie in the process of grooming. Men in senior positions tend to act as patrons to younger men: encouraging them, providing them with relevant information, suggesting them for assignments which will broaden their range of experiences. In short, they help them in ways that either do not occur to them to offer to women or that they would not feel comfortable about offering (see Kanter, 1977). Any attempt to quantify such relationships would reduce to trivia the nature of the interaction (lunch four times a month and three telephone calls a week). Similarly, any attempt to have senior men lunch with younger women four times a month and telephone them three times a week might signify an entirely different type of relationship. And if we cannot quantify, do we exclude as inconvenient and dismiss as irrelevant?

The production of numbers should not be an end in itself but the emphasis on survey and resurvey to produce masses of numbers over very short periods of time looks perilously like an end. Neither does a change in numbers over surveys necessarily mean that the processes have changed in the desired direction. As Ronalds comments:

> When an employer sends a report to the government agency, the agency can not know whether the 12 women apprentices shown on the form are the 10 shown the year before, plus two new recruits, or whether the previous 10 were all sacked or all left, and this is a totally new group: or whether the 12 are a mixture. (1987a:34)

Leaving aside the question of whether anybody actually checks for accuracy the numbers provided by organisations (it took a long time for the numbers of Cyril Burt to be revealed as somewhat less than accurate), an obsession with numbers is likely to sidetrack analysts into examining the minutiae of a mere tool of analysis.

Some problems with State intervention

There is one problem which cannot simply be dismissed as libertarian opposition to state intervention. It is that the state, in arrogating these powers and investing them in particular bureaucratic sections, funnels the processes of affirmative action in ways which may not originally have been envisaged, at least by the people whom it is in principle meant to serve. These issues themselves may undergo some transformations and the question 'Who stands to gain what from the exercise?' invites unexpected answers. Which sections of the migrant community, Aboriginal society or women in Australia reap the benefits, and in what ways? The point is that state intervention, in effecting social change, is reliant on bureaucratic processes and thus, no matter how apparently viable or desirable that intervention (or perhaps even how impracticable or unwelcome), it is subject to attenuation and to reshaping. The result is that outcomes may not be wholly congruent with intentions. This is inevitably the case, even when the bureaucratic processes through which affirmative action is directed themselves remain relatively constant, and even more likely when they do not.

Then the chances of present actions producing unforeseen, unintended and at times undesirable consequences are multiplied.

By no means does this critical approach cast state intervention as inappropriate or undesirable. Historically the state has had a critical role to play in accelerating social change. It does seem necessary, however, to be alert to the likelihood of unintended and possibly undesirable consequences:

> We would certainly do well to heed the observation that the bureaucracy perceives itself as the ultimate purpose of the state, passing off form as content and content as form. For in this way the purposes of the state are transformed into purposes of office and vice-versa. (Marx [1843] in Coletti, 1975:107)

4

Bastards

Being a discussion of some of the forms that resistance to EEO change takes and of who resists and why.

Social change and concepts with either a hidden or overt agenda of social change do not emerge Athena-like in a fully fledged and resolved form and at a single and identifiable social moment. It is a question of process in which the interaction of social forces is constantly reforming ideation and behaviour.

The concept of equality of opportunity is premised on the need for social change. Yet since society, and our understanding of it, is ever shifting, so is our understanding of what we mean by equality of opportunity, or at least our perception of its application. The fundamental argument is that citizens of a democratic society should enjoy equal opportunities to achieve the same political, economic and social conditions. This theme has constancy. What has changed is the understanding of who is considered citizen and who, therefore, is eligible to share these opportunities. Looking at More's *Utopia* we can see that social divisions are to be eliminated in that ideal state and equality will prevail. There was no question, however, that this equalising be extended to slaves, who remained outside society, and although women were expected to contribute their labour to the state this was over and above their domestic contribution; nor did it lessen their domestic subjugation. Today, Pateman (1985) argues that while women and men have a civil status which is formally equal, in practice women have not yet achieved citizenship in the same sense as have men. What it is that should be shared, the social conditions, has become more closely defined and identified, as indeed Pateman's argument points up. To have the vote, for example, is crucial but it is not all, as enfranchised but in many other ways disadvantaged Australian citizens would attest. Again, to have the same formal right to education and employment as members of other groups in the society is a basic and critical right. But if, for a battery of other reasons relating to values, attitudes and social structures, such education or employment is seldom attainable, at least not in the same

57

forms and to the same degree, then having the formal right is a hollow entitlement.

Just as slaves were never perceived as members of the (dominant) society, so were Aborigines outcast as Australian citizens in democratic white Australia. It is chastening to remember that Aborigines were disenfranchised until the late 1960s, and it is a long way from the truth to suggest that today they enjoy the same social conditions, or opportunities to achieve them, as non-Aboriginal Australians. Furthermore, for all that women in Australia won the vote in 1902, they have certainly not won the struggle for equality of opportunity (see *inter alia* Baldock and Cass, 1983; Sawer, 1984). Over the years there has, however, been a change in attitudes and a change in the material conditions of existence and the opportunities open to those who were previously much more disadvantaged members of society. This does not mean to say that equality of opportunity has been achieved, because as each 'minority' group has claimed the same right of access to social benefits and responsibilities as other 'full' members of society, opposition to those claims has welled from other sectors in the community. It has indeed been and continues as a struggle for women to improve their social, economic and political position and for members of migrant groups to be accepted into the society. It is a struggle to win recognition of the fact that Aborigines have a just claim for a very different social treatment, and then to have it accorded. It is also a struggle to check the attitudinal spill-over endured by physically disabled people who, suffering a particular disability, may then have foisted on them an assumption of general incapacity — it is a bizarre response to believe that someone who cannot, say, walk or hear is unable to perform normally in other respects.

At the historical point when there is formal and even majority support for social changes proposed to improve the circumstances and opportunities of disadvantaged members of the society, it nonetheless seems inevitable that hostile and reactive voices will continue to be raised. This is patently clear in the context of reducing inequality of opportunities. Formalised approaches to developing equal opportunity policies and more particularly to implementing equal opportunity practices have met with a number of forms of resistance from a number of people and for a number of reasons.

Forms of resistance

At the developmental stage, resistance to EEO can take a variety of forms: from disbelief, ignorance and misrepresentation to more full-blooded attempts to generate fear of the consequences of the enactment of the legislation. Once legislation has been enacted, outright refusal to comply is unusual. Nonetheless resistance may be expressed in a variety of ways, none of which is openly acknowledged.

Sustained disbelief

Perhaps one of the most elementary forms of resistance to change is to avow that change is not necessary; that is, either the system does not shelter discrimination or alternatively people are content with the way things are. It is also an early response to claims that, for whatever reason, change is desirable. The fact that there is no formal or overt barrier to the achievement of certain positions or benefits is presented as sufficient argument for maintaining the *status quo*. The assertion is made that access is open to all who want to pursue that particular goal — it is a matter of qualifications and will. That some members of disadvantaged groups have achieved is advanced as proof positive of the openness and egalitarian nature of the system. The claim is premised on the belief that if these people succeeded, then so can others.

In Australia we do indeed have female professors in universities (they constitute, however, but three per cent of the professoriate) and we do have Aborigines in senior bureaucratic positions (relatively fewer than female professors, we suspect) but in no way can this be construed as meaning that these positions are as accessible to women and Aborigines as they are to white Australian males. Even allowing for the fact that the professoriate and the bureaucracy may not be attractive worlds for many Aborigines and women, such a suggestion is risible. At best sustained disbelief is characterised by social myopia and naivete. In other senses it is dishonest.

Disbelief can be remarkably selective. Some universities, for example, acknowledge that discrimination is a problem for society, but find it hard to believe that it could possibly exist in the liberal, enlightened environment attributed to academe. Perhaps somewhat differently, some private sector companies, while supporting EEO programs, did not believe that legislation was necessary — at least as far as they were concerned. Indeed, several of those companies participated in the Commonwealth Government's Affirmative Action Pilot Program precisely in order to extend their own disbelief to the Government.

Ignorance

Often underlying sustained disbelief, and indeed other forms of resistance to change, is some measure of ignorance of what actually constitutes discrimination. In this context ignorance is not necessarily

adequately covered by a dictionary definition such as want of knowledge, learning or information. Even so, non-understanding or un-
awareness of what discrimination is, how it works and how it is
manifest is common enough. After all, why should people 'know' if
they have not been educated in the matter or attuned to the problem
and so be able to observe it. In the circumstances of what might be
termed simple ignorance it is possible, sometimes even easy, to move
the hearts and minds of people of goodwill. More problematical and
recalcitrant is wilful and persistent ignorance. This is evident when
the problem, and the language which has been developed in the
course of analysis of the problem, have been well and perhaps frequently explained, but when resistance to the notion of change in the
elimination of discrimination is deeply entrenched. Then, it seems, no
matter how good or how intense the educational program, understanding of discrimination and the injustice of it will not gain so much
as a toehold.

Ignorance can persist beyond the point of enactment of legislation.
The New South Wales Anti-Discrimination Board embarked upon a
community education program designed to explain what exactly constituted unlawful discrimination. Leaflets, presentations and publicity
for decisions of the Board and the Equal Opportunity Tribunal continued 'without penalty' for the first eight years after the enactment of
the legislation. After that, the Tribunal offered a further incentive to
employers to renounce their state of ignorance — it began to award
financial damages to complainants against employers.

Misrepresentation

Ignorance, as simple lack of knowledge, may deform accounts or
analyses of inequality of opportunity, but, so long as it is not a
question of ill-will, the task of sorting out the difficulties is not in-
surmountable. Deliberate misrepresentation is, however, a practical
outcome of wilful and persistent ignorance. It distorts both the
methods proposed to correct inequitable practices and arguments
about the injustice of certain social relationships. An argot has been
developed in association with affirmative action and the disfigure-
ments of these words are instances of this ploy. It is a tactic also
applied to the concepts. Despite explanations and definitions of usage,
deliberately confounding goals, targets and forward estimates with
quotas is a good example of how words can be used to manipulate.
Fundamental thinking suffers no less from misrepresentation; for
example, on a visit to Australia from the United States of America, a
vigorous critic of equality of opportunity averred that the philosophy
of affirmative action is 'redress...women got it in the neck for

thousands of years, isn't it time men suffered?' (Levin, quoted in *Sydney Morning Herald*, 15 August 1984.)

Provoking Alarm

Whipping up fear has always been a political weapon wielded by opponents of change. It works best when it is simple-minded and emotive, invoking words and slogans which link what is currently being debated to universally recognised bogeymen of the past: the left labels proposals fascist, the right labels them Stalinist. The Senate debate on the Commonwealth Affirmative Action Bill provides some worthy contributions to this genre. On the one hand there is reference to the pall of mediocrity which will overcome society if equality of opportunity, which it is alleged actually means equality of outcome, prevails. On the other there is offered the spectre of what happened in Iran when the Shah sought to emancipate women—a revival of Islamic fundamentalism! (Senate, 22 August 1986.)

Obstructionism

Obstructionism can be either active or passive. Active obstructionism is evident when there are conscious efforts to divert benefits from flowing to the disadvantaged and to return them to the already privileged. It occurs, for example, when women answering all formal requirements for a job are not appointed, allegedly because of a lack of toilet facilities. As an argument against appointing women this is basically weak, but it has often been used effectively and indeed continues to be trotted out. Albeit less directly, it is active obstructionism when alterations and additions to the buildings of a workplace are being carried out yet there is no provision made for toilets that women might use. The argument at the time might be that there are no women working there, but it establishes a means of ensuring that women's employment at future times will be problematical. In this second instance the obstructionism is active because steps are deliberately taken to exclude a set of people from future employment.

In passive obstructionism no steps are actually taken, rather change is subverted by inaction and the *status quo* is preserved. In this sense inaction is set against an awareness of the circumstances and a capacity to act but a determination not to (see Lukes, 1974). It is not that questions relating perhaps to conditions discriminating against women, or unequal educational opportunities for Aborigines, are addressed and then rejected as being capable or worthy of change (although this may occur), rather that these questions are not addressed in the first place. They do not appear on the agenda as items for consideration. Yet there are cases when they do have this visibility and then, no matter what decisions are made, nothing is done. The weight of the system seems to grind matters to a halt.

Circumvention

Circumvention of the requirements of equal employment opportunity legislation differs from obstructionism. It implies getting around the requirement as opposed to blocking it. Jewson and Mason (1986a) identify two types. 'Circumvention by neglect' occurs, for example, where a commitment to the policies is announced — there may even be a claim to participation in publicly heralded programs — but this is not actively prosecuted and translated into specific actions (see Benokraitis and Feagin, 1978:39,83). The neglect is less benign when individual employees are made responsible for implementing the program — but it is in addition to their normal duties which always have to take precedence and which absorb all their energies and time. Competing priorities are real threats to many EEO programs. In the public sector funding cuts, the twin gods of efficiency and effectiveness, and obeying the new managerialist imperatives have many higher education institutions and public service departments so absorbed in fighting to save what constitutes their *raison d'être* that EEO can quite easily be relegated to the status of a niggling worry. From time to time it seeps into the consciousness, but its weighed under again very easily by more pressing problems. According to Jewson and Mason it is 'circumvention by manipulation' when formal rules are scrupulously followed but in such a way as to maintain the bias of the system. Members of the disadvantaged groups may realise that there has been some sleight of hand but be unable to identify it precisely. Or worse, they may be able to specify exactly how the trick was done but be unable to protest. This is clearly the case when constant use is made on selection and promotions committees of the same token woman who happens to be antagonistic to the appointment and promotion of other women. Formal requirements are met but it can safely be assumed that the woman will not be sympathetic to, or may even be hostile to, female applicants.

The requirement in the Commonwealth legislation for consultation with unions and employees, particularly women employees, provides wonderful opportunities for delay and watering down of proposals. If there are complaints about the delays, the complainants can be referred to the law. Collegiate decision-making processes characteristic of universities are most useful for this purpose. A draft policy originating in one form from one committee is put on the merry-go-round of other committees and interested parties for comment and feedback. The draft is amended to take often contradictory comments into account and put back onto the merry-go-round for comment on the amended draft. And so on.

Nor are universities alone in their ability to use consultative processes for purposes other than their ostensible one, as this extract from *Yes Prime Minister* illustrates:

'. . .And with respect, Prime Minister, I think you should know that the DES will react with some caution to this rather novel proposal. . .'
I stayed calm. 'So you think they'll block it?'
'I mean', he said, tight-lipped and angry, 'that they will give it the most serious and urgent consideration, but will insist on a thorough and rigorous examination of all the proposals, allied to a detailed feasibility study and budget analysis before producing a consultative document for consideration by all interested bodies and seeking comments and recommendations to be incorporated in a brief for a series of working parties who will produce individual studies that will form the background for a more wideranging document considering whether or not the proposal should be taken forward to the next stage.'
He meant they'd block it! (Lynn and Jay, 1989:479)

Institutional inertia

While not formally resistant to the creation of equality of opportunity, institutional inertia may easily exhaust any such initiatives. Although inertia may overtake matters already stagnating because of benign neglect it differs from this form of inattention because it may simply be a question of allowing established procedures to take their full course (or not). The very weight of the bureaucracy can thus crush them or alternatively provide the means for reducing their potency. Prevarication and resorting to delaying tactics can often enough throw proposed change into the slough of institutional inertia where it may bog or even disappear. Wilenski refers to resistance through the tyranny of detail. The argument is that in large and complex bureaucracies broad policy decisions must be able to be understood and applied in all sections and at all levels of the institution. He writes that in order to comply with the original intent of the decision 'continual interpretation and reinterpretation by officials must take place' (1982:38). Not only does this procedure allow for 'natural' attrition of the proposed change, it positively accommodates subversion.

Wilenski also refers to resistance through delay; indeed, the case may be made for the need to take time 'to study matters, refer matters to committees, consult with outside groups, conduct surveys, seek additional information' (1982:40) and the like. Whatever the ruse, it postpones the moment of change. It may even be that the proposed change is held in abeyance until the impetus is lost or the circumstances so altered that the change loses its relevance, or is too difficult or else is forgotten. Delay, of course, may be quite openly advocated and the argument then is not that the proposed reform is unacceptable, it is the timing. In 1908 Cornford wrote:

> The Principle of Unripe Time is that people should not do at the present moment what they think right at that moment, because the moment at which they think it right has not yet arrived...Time, by the way, is like the medlar; it has a trick of going rotten before it is ripe. (1949 [1908]:16)

Trenchant critiques of obvious obduracy in attitudes towards change have been offered, tellingly, in the form of satirical checklists for action or nonaction. In lampooning tactical resistance the checklists identify and simultaneously disparage the various reactive strategies. It can be an elegant and entertaining exercise. The following catalogue has as its target universities. With little modification the points are equally as barbed in other bureaucratic contexts. Most indicate, despite a level of personalism, how obstructionism can shelter in the behaviours of bureaucracy and what could be termed institutional artifice.

Fifty ways of avoiding change: a checklist for saving time and ingenuity.

1   We have already tried it.
2   The department of X has already tried it.
3   We have never tried anything like that before.
4   I know of no department that has ever tried that.
5   We haven't the money.
6   We haven't the time.
7   We haven't suitable staff.
8   We would want to do it but the students could be upset by it.
9   I would like to but the Vice-Chancellor (Dean, Professor, technicians, secretaries, tea lady) would never stand for it.
10 That is no doubt suitable in industry but universities aren't like that.
11 It's an American idea isn't it?
12 I can see it would be better in the long run but I have got too much on my plate at present to contemplate any change.
13 We've got a better idea.
14 But our University doesn't work like that.
15 I'd just never get it through.
16 Not if it means another committee.

17 We have turned down similar ideas before.
18 It's immoral.
19 It's too altruistic.
20 It's alright in theory but...
21 It's not intellectually respectable.
22 Who are you to suggest ideas?
23 I'm wanted on the other line.
24 Yes we should talk about it, I have my diary here, how about next July?
25 That infringes academic freedom.
26 They all have tenure, how else could we employ them?
27 Yes, when we get into our new building.
28 Well the chair is vacant at present, perhaps when that has been filled.
29 You don't understand our set up.
30 I haven't had a chance to read your suggestions properly but it seems to me...
31 ...but it's the first year of the quinquennium.
32 ...but it's the last year of the quinquennium.
33 Above all I must cover the syllabus.
34 We are a community of scholars, we don't have a policy as such.
35 Well now let's see, I'm not sure which committee that should go through.
36 I must say your premises fascinate me.
37 But didn't I read a paper by Eysenck (Ashby, Carter, Halsey) in which he argues...
38 You should read our report on...
39 Ho! Ho! I must say you're optimistic.
40 I'm sure you're right but I'm retiring next year.
41 Look, the whole thing's going to be different in five years time anyway.
42 Well you know it's largely a matter of swings and roundabouts.
43 We are waiting on the report of the Oakes (James, NUS, Fulton) Committee.
44 We hope to make an appointment of someone who could look after this kind of thing in 19xx.
45 It's your jargon I can't stand.
46 You are what they call an ergonome chappie aren't you?
47 I can think of many ways in which the finance could be spent to more advantage.
48 It would be unfortunate if the notion gained currency that formal instruction was necessary in order to become a university teacher.
49 *A fortium* these proposals have no place in the universities.
50 The proposal did not raise sufficient support within the university. (Piper and Glatter, 1977:408−409)

Kanter too lists a set of 'rules for stifling innovation', that is, ways of blocking change. She sees them as the response we might associate with segmentalist organisation where the style of management, by compartmentalising issues and actions, makes it unattractive and difficult for employees to seek to institute change. The segmenting approach contains problems. It keeps ideas and actions in isolation. The hierarchical form of bureaucracy is maintained but the functional units hold separate. Kanter offers following ten points as something of a credo of segmentalism:

1 Regard any new idea from below with suspicion — because it's new, and because it's from below.
2 Insist that people who need your approval to act first go through several other levels of management to get their signatures.
3 Ask departments or individuals to challenge and criticise each other's proposals. (That saves you the job of deciding; you just pick the survivor.)
4 Express your criticisms freely, and withhold your praise. (That keeps people on their toes.) Let them know they can be fired at any time.
5 Treat identification of problems as signs of failure, to discourage people from letting you know when something in their area isn't working.
6 Control everything carefully. Make sure people count anything that can be counted, frequently.
7 Make decisions to reorganise or change policies in secret, and spring them on people unexpectedly. (That also keeps them on their toes.)
8 Make sure that requests for information are fully justified, and make sure that it is not given out to managers freely. (You don't want data falling into the wrong hands.)
9 Assign lower-level managers, in the name of delegation and participation, responsibility for figuring out how to cut back, lay off, move people around, or otherwise implement threatening decisions you have made. And get them to do it quickly.
10 And above all, never forget that you, the higher-ups, already know everything important about this business. (Kanter, 1983:101)

Who resists?

It is not possible to plot resistance along single-stranded lines of men as opposed to women, of Australian-born as opposed to migrants, of the powerful as opposed to the powerless. Resistance erupts from many loci, although it is possible to identify certain classes of resistance. It is certainly located in the authority structure; despite endeavours on the part of some committed individuals and even a number

of formal gestures by organisations themselves, not to mention legislation covering some of these organisations, there is more than a hint
of resistance at this level.

The reluctance, even failure, on the part of some government
departments and statutory authorities in New South Wales to bring
forward a management plan as required of them under the legislation
must be interpreted as a form of resistance. But relatively powerless,
disadvantaged people and groups may themselves resist changes
directed towards creating equality of opportunity. This is perhaps
harder to understand. Why should disadvantaged workers be anti-
pathetic to measures which are likely to result in structural changes
improving their job opportunities and opening career paths? Why
should female secretaries or migrant labourers resist?

It is not only that uninterest, antipathy or even hostility cannot be
plotted clearly according to organisational power relationships — these
responses do not fall out neatly along the lines of ethnic background
or gender either. Many women who are struggling unequally against
economic or other social pressures, as well as those with high hopes of
success and the already successful, support changes directed to creating
equality of opportunity. Yet there are others who do not. And so it is
with people from different cultural backgrounds. The full spectrum of
responses can be represented. Although poaching on the following
section (Why Resist?), it is somewhat easier to understand, even to
identify, who resists by reference to reasons for resisting. One very
good reason may be an identified deficiency of the proposed programs.
They might appear quite irrelevant to some individuals and groups or
they might be crass in their formulation and implementation — in
other words, the suggested means of achieving what might be accepted as desirable changes gives offence and/or offers no real hope.
There are other possible reasons.

In a tight labour market it is not surprising that workers in, say, a
previously male-dominated industry or occupation should resent the
incursion of women. Equalising opportunity is seen to be directly
contrary to their immediate interests. Any group which has had some
control over its own conditions of existence, in employment or any
other realm, is likely to be displeased if asked or required to relinquish
or loosen that control — especially when it includes control over the
flow and direction of advantages and returns. The apparently determined lack of interest by the North Australian Workers Union, and
over many decades, in the depressed conditions of Aboriginal workers
on cattle stations in the Northern Territory and ambiguous support
for them even when the Union was under pressure to extend that
support (see Stevens, 1974:159−160, 189−205) is an example of such
interest-directed behaviour.

Dominant ideologies may also prompt people who would stand to gain from particular social changes to resist them. Thus some women, entrenchedly socialised in a view of gender roles and relationships which transforms difference to disadvantage, may interpret moves for change as against society and against nature. In a good many cases, class position is a potentially significant variable in reviewing resistance. Privilege may well promote an intransigent attitude to change but, as we have indicated, relatively underprivileged members of society can also look askance at such suggestions. The importance of class relationships is often overlooked in analysis because, while it is not necessarily so, power and privilege are likely to dull understanding of the weight and extent of difficulties confronting people disadvantaged in the class system. That is, the observers themselves bring bias.

It is not only a matter of class blindness in analysis (at least this does not inevitably imply hostility). It is also a case of implacable opposition to the notion of equality on the part of some people whose progress has been paved by privilege. This argument boils down to a belief in aptitude and application, that is, if individuals are competent and willing they can succeed. No matter that due to their class position opportunities (for example, education) necessary in the first instance for success even to be a possibility were foreclosed. No matter that the conventional wisdom of our society attributes lesser abilities to some categories of people, particularly in behaviour associated with highly valued social performances; an attribution which limits their chance of success, thereby becoming a self-fulfilling prophecy. No matter that actually the demands are likely to be heavier for some; Aboriginal people, for instance, may well have to work harder than whites to achieve certain positions, not because of any lesser ability but because they have to demonstrate to white gatekeepers that they have more. Basically the argument of the already successful is that whatever the circumstances people can pull themselves up by their own bootstraps — no matter that they are barefoot. It is also true that their social class position may imbue the disadvantaged with a sense of the irrelevance of EEO programs for them. The reality of their existence prompts extreme circumspection, even cynicism, for their experiences lead them to believe that their expectations must be of struggle — and that unaided. To cite an extreme view: how can a system designed to give improved promotion prospects assist those people who are chronically unemployed?

Why resist?

In some instances the answer could be apathy. First and foremost it rests on some level of awareness, albeit minimal, of the nature and circumstances of disadvantage. Quite obviously there cannot be apathy in total ignorance. But apathy must also be set against one or other (or combinations) of the following responses: that the issue is perceived as inconsequential; that the issue is not really regarded as legitimate; and that the issue has no implications at a personal level. That is, apathy can only result from distancing oneself from the issue or diminishing it. As we have observed, for some there is a sense of hopelessness about equality of opportunity ever becoming a reality. Their appraisal of their own social position is such that they cannot believe in what must seem like miracles. Any change likely to be produced is perceived to be quite remote in its effect and without personal consequences of any moment.

In some instances conservatism may be a result of apathy. It is surely less demanding to do nothing and for many, even those who stand to benefit from change, to stay with an established set of relationships and expectations provides a feeling of greater security and comfort than moving towards a less predictable, even unknown future. The stress in conservatism is on the present, but a present legitimated by its past. Present arrangements are affirmed by their historical forms being in continuation, not in transcendence. Social forms and behaviours may thus be advanced as having inherent value simply because they are: they can then be celebrated and legitimated in traditional terms. Yet, as Mannheim points out, there are dangers in the steadfastly backward gaze and uncritical endorsement of that which exists simply because it exists, since 'conservative quietism tends to justify, by irrational means, everything that exists at all' (1940:211). Moreover, reference to present arrangements and to history needs to be somewhat selective. For example, the position of women in the nuclear family, the very nub of our social structure, is not only unquestioningly accepted as traditional but a tradition stretching back even beyond history. It is true that some form of sexual division of labour appears as a cultural and historical constant, although what women do and what men do varies from society to society. More than that, however, the idealised domestic setting of women in a nuclear family has only had saliency since the end of the eighteenth century (see Davidoff *et al*, 1976). Not only is it limited to capitalist countries, even then it is not an ideal which has practically incorporated working class women.

Perhaps the most critical factor in working towards a response to the question 'why resist?' is that of interests. As Kaufman observes, people on both sides of the social change fence are animated by self-interest. Those who feel deprived would generally hope to see relationships reconstituted while those who are advantaged by present arrangements would seek to retain those forms (1971:44).

The notion of interests, however, can take one of a number of forms of various complexity and operational adequacy (Connolly, 1972); in all instances it is 'irreducibly evaluative' (Lukes, 1974:34). Whatever the understanding of the notion it remains a central consideration in analysis of why some individuals and groups resist change designed to improve social opportunities for others. While discussion of interests inevitably broaches questions of preferences, wants and needs, we should open it up to take account of systemic bias. This is significant because people's 'wants may themselves be a product of a system which works against their interests, and in such cases, relates the latter to what they would want and prefer, were they able to make the choice' (Lukes, 1974:34; see also Connolly, 1972:472). The notion of interests is comparative; the interests of one particular group or individual are set against and indeed are often contrary to the interests of others. What people anticipate, or perhaps have experienced as the outcome of certain policies or practices, will shape their identification of their interests and endeavours to advance and protect them.

Consensus may be sought as a means of tapping diverse views and making certain social changes with a minimum of socially dislocating consequences. To seek consensus is to recognise a range of potentially competing interests and to accommodate them with some sort of best fit. Paradoxically it may do little more than provide a vehicle for power play and the subjugation of classes of interests. While consensus is represented as an operative principle of the democratic spirit, a means of decision-making in the general interest, to make it a necessary goal may also be a way to diminish, or at least postpone, certain social changes. The point is that it is believed to be important to demonstrate that consensus prevails at the highest levels. The actual voices of the powerless may not be heard or heeded. Not only do their interests stand to be under represented, perhaps ignored, but the desire for consensus is basically a fear of rocking the boat.

Inevitably change carries a threat of disruption. Those who have the power to implement change may resist for two reasons. Firstly, people advantaged by the bias of a system would be reluctant to advocate a shift in that bias away from their interest. Secondly, they may fear criticism of their leadership for not securing social stability. Widening the field of candidates for jobs improves the chances of creating a pool of better qualified and more talented applicants from which to make the most appropriate appointment for any position. This is one of the arguments for introducing equality of opportunity programs, that is, it is in the interests of management and efficiency. While this is so, we must also acknowledge that in widening the field we are likely to reduce individual chances, particularly the chances of the less well qualified. Thus, improving the employment opportunities for women can be, and is, construed as limiting them for men. In

times of economic buoyancy, when unemployment figures are generally
low, the labour market can absorb new recruits without stirring
resentment—or at least the criticism is more difficult to sustain.
During recessions, however, or simply in times of stagnation, the
argument gathers force. Reference is made to unemployment figures
for men and poignant stories are recounted of unemployed white
Australian-born family men. That the fearful economic, social and
psychological consequences of unemployment are experienced by the
young and the old, as well as the middle-aged, by women as well as
men, by migrants no less than Australian-born, certainly most de-
structively by Aborigines, and as a double burden for disabled people, is
not acknowledged. The traditional model of the nuclear family with a
male breadwinner and household head, and a wife and mother locked
into a state of domestic dependence, is unquestioningly advanced as
the ideal—given and immutable. An ideology of female dependence
and white-australocentrism provide grounds for bitter criticism of
women, Aborigines and migrants who are identified competitors in
the labour market. An article in a newsletter of Women Who Want to
be Women rails against middle-aged women 'costing thousands of
teenage boys a chance of a career in the West Australian Public
Service' (1985:9). In this case the alleged victims are potential fathers
who need to establish a career, the villains not simply women but
middle-aged women—that group which in traditional terms should be
at home and dependent, not seeking to follow careers on their own
behalf. It is indeed not merely women, but specifically married
women, who bear the brunt of criticism for their efforts to establish
their economic and social independence. It is difficult to disregard
completely the zero sum nature of the employment/unemployment
argument although it short-circuits the question of qualifications and
ability. The same finite quality, however, also colours views of the
availability of other benefits. To some degree there may be limits on
the numbers of promotions to particular positions in any organisation,
whilever they retain their pyramidal structure, or to educational
places in institutions, although an argument of direct displacement,
which discounts the relevance of qualifications, is even more difficult
to sustain. But when we come to contemplate other benefits claimed
principally by, and often reserved for, members of dominant groups
there is no reason to believe they constitute a limited resource. Burton,
for example, says:

> I do not believe, from my observations and experience, that
> within work organisations power, influence and opportunity exist
> in finite quantities. Kanter supports the view that games which
> are played around them are not zero sum in nature. Part of the
> fear of change is the belief that they are. (1984:97)

Resistance to the changes required if equality of opportunity is to become a reality is clear in the attitudes of some individual members of disadvantaged groups who have, for a variety of reasons, been able to overcome systemic barriers. This is very much in line with Banks' contention that 'there have always been prominent women to argue an anti-feminist cause' (1981:247). But who are these women? And again the question why?

Abramson (1975) examines the unsympathetic response of some women in academe towards other women struggling to succeed. She invokes the term 'Queen Bees', coined by Staines *et al* (1974), in referring to women who have succeeded in their field and who fervidly deny there is systemic discrimination against women in the society. The reasoning behind the rejection is tied to their perception, and defence, of their own achievement, their talent and their effort. According to Abramson's study, the successful were

> all too willing to adopt the attitudes that, since they made it
> through the system, anyone who has not made it just does not
> have the ability to compete. To recognize that discrimination is a
> major factor in the system would be, for these women, to
> invalidate their own deeply felt conviction that they, at least, are
> meritorious and merit usually wins out. (1975:116)

In other words, Queen Bees feel that to concede that some people are likely to be unsuccessful because of bias in the system would be to devalue their own efforts and attainments. Typically, they have worked hard to succeed and see no reason why other women should not go through the same hoops (Staines, 1974:57) Queen Bees are also likely to consider other women to have less ability or to be less motivated, even downright lazy — attitudes which put their own achievements into higher relief. Further, they strongly endorse the dominant system of values because it is the frame for their achievement which will doubtless be premised on ability but may also have been helped along by class relationships and even by sheer luck. This is also the general storyline for men although, as men, they have a distinct edge in opportunities in this society. There is no evidence that the Queen Bee syndrome should be transposed in analysis of other social categories which are relatively disadvantaged. There is no suggestion, for example, that successful Aborigines claim that any Aborigine with talent and will can forge ahead equally well. And despite, or in this instance perhaps because of, the huge class differences and various ethnic origins and levels of success in their new country, prospering people from different cultural backgrounds do not adopt such a simple-minded, self-congratulatory posture. Some successful people certainly argue that on the basis of their achievements others can achieve similarly—if they try. But unlike Queen Bees they do not claim that there is no discrimination, rather that they surmounted it.

The homosociobility argument has assumed some centrality to analyses of resistance to equal opportunity proposals. The central notion extends the idea that people are more comfortable with, and therefore seek, others who are 'their kind' to encompass the way that these people ensure that the power and privilege they enjoy at work are the preserve of others with similar social characteristics. Thus if people do not possess the attributes traditionally manifest by those occupying certain positions, they are deemed inappropriate for those positions. In this way, and as Kanter so succinctly writes, 'the men who manage reproduce themselves in kind' (Kanter, 1977:48). This behaviour is always designed to monopolise benefits and as such is a form of social closure (see Parkin, 1974). It is a clear example of how two modes of social closure, exclusion and solidarism, are used in complementary fashion to achieve a tight grip on opportunities and claims to benefits. Although Moore in kindly terms described the organisational relationships established in this system of social reproduction as a 'bureaucratic kinship system' (1962:109) and recognised its attraction, he was quite alert to its less attractive nepotistic features.

Burton records (1984:94) that the homosociobility argument has been advanced, albeit under different tags, for a number of decades. In her analysis she develops the notion that it is the masculine style of some work which makes it attractive to men; not only more comfortable, but more rewarding generally. In some cases the masculine connotation derives from no more than the fact that men do it, although how it is done and when it is done are also important considerations. In all events, if women take up that work it becomes devalued. It is, as we pointed out in Chapter 2, even possible to attach a cost in money to the degree of devaluation. Such a threat is averted by means of homosocial reproduction. Analysis of this form of closure is not, however, confined to the field of gender relationships. Hughes describes with clarity how it also perpetuates racial and ethnic divisions and disadvantage (1944). Insofar as homosocial reproduction rests on the significance attached to certain characteristics which are the self-defining characteristics of the dominant group, then it is not surprising that it 'leaves women out, along with a range of other people with discrepant social characteristics' (Kanter, 1977:68).

The point is that people of like background, outlook and interests trust each other, at least more than they trust people from other social milieux. They recognise their commonality and value its principles and practices. They thus confirm the rightness of their attitudes and celebrate their personal achievement. When gatekeepers exercise their powers in favour of people cast in their own image they ensure the smooth continuation of the *status quo* important for organisational stability and control of uncertainty.

Perhaps Cornford (1949) provides the most incisive summary of recalcitrance in attitudes to change. He writes:

> There is only one argument for doing something, the rest are arguments for doing nothing.
>
> The argument for doing something is that it is the right thing to do. But then, of course, comes the difficulty of making sure that it is right. (14)

But what are the arguments for doing nothing? Cornford gives the following as rules of inaction:

> 1. The Principle of the Wedge applies when it is not possible to prove that an action is unjust. It points out the dangers of acting justly in the first instance for you may be expected, unreasonably, to act, perhaps even more justly, in the future.
> 2. The Priciple of the Dangerous Precedent, which is akin to the Principle of the Wedge, again postulates that it is unwise to act properly now for fear that you will not have the courage to do so in the future. Actions which are not customary are therefore wrong and precedent dangerous.
> 3. The Fair Trial Argument is self-explanatory. Since change is to be deplored the Fair Trial Argument applies specifically to existing systems, not proposed changes. Essentially the message is — the present system deserves a 'fair go', give it longer.
> 4. The Principle of Unripe Time, [to which we have already referred], advances that people should not do at the present moment what they think right at that moment, because the moment at which they think it right has not yet arrived.

And again, it is important to point out that time, like the medlar, '...has a trick of going rotten before it is ripe' (16).

5

Beneficiaries

Being an examination of the promises of benefits that would flow from EEO, the benefits delivered, to whom and at what cost.

Cato, that great and grave philosopher, did commonly demand, when a new project was propounded unto him, *cui bono*, what good will ensue in case the same is effected. (Brewer, 1983:298)

In one form or another equal opportunity legislation has been enacted in most states in Australia, the exceptions being Queensland and Tasmania. National coverage is afforded in some areas by Commonwealth legislation which applies to all states and territories. The most visible and contested form of equal opportunity legislation is that which applies to employment; here New South Wales has the longest history with the state public services operating under EEO since 1980. It is timely to ask, 'What good has ensued?' from these programs. What exactly is the nature of the benefit that they seek to bestow and on whom are they envisaged as bestowing it?

Who will benefit

When the New South Wales Premier introduced the Anti-Discrimination (Amendment) Bill into the Legislative Assembly in March 1980 he claimed three major benefits for the Equal Employment Opportunity provisions which comprised it: social justice, increased efficiency and effectiveness of administration, and a more representative public service. The then Leader of the Opposition criticised a number of aspects of the legislation but did not dispute the forecast benefits. The Government Leader in the Legislative Council stressed how EEO, by increasing career opportunities, would lead to improved job performance (New South Wales Parliamentary Debates, Hansard, 1980, Vol CLIII:5496−7, Vol CLIV:6241).

Thus from the outset in New South Wales Equal Employment Opportunity was seen as a means to several ends only one of which, and a minor one at that, was a very particular notion of a more just society. More important was the belief that it would lead to improved job performance by individual public servants, and a more representative bureaucracy both of which would in turn lead to an overall increase in the efficiency and effectiveness of the service and better delivery of services.

The New South Wales *Affirmative Action Handbook* reaffirms these benefits. Little or no effort is directed toward explaining to the intended beneficiaries of the legislation, named unfortunately but perhaps appropriately enough 'target groups', what is in it for them. They are assumed to want what the legislation intends to bestow upon them: increased job performance, raised career expectations and freedom of choice 'within the constraints of available employment'. They appear not to have been consulted prior to the introduction of the legislation which itself provides no role for consultation after enactment. EEO is quited clearly defined in the New South Wales legislation as a management issue.

Very similar messages about who benefits prefigure the design of EEO Programs in the Commonwealth Public Service (see Joint Subcommittee on Women in the Service, 1984:7).

The impression that EEO/AA is a new managerial imperative to be imposed on beneficiaries comes through very strongly in the three government publications surrounding the Commonwealth Government's Affirmative Action Pilot Program for Women: *Affirmative Action for Women Policy Discussion Paper* (May 1984), Affirmative Action for Women — A *Progress Report on the Pilot Program. July 1984 to May 1985* (May 1985) and Working Party on Affirmative Action Legislation — *Report* (September 1985). While it could be argued that because the Pilot Program sought the voluntary participation of 28 private sector employers and three higher education institutions the benefits to management of the participating organisations had to be played up and those to beneficiaries underplayed, there are dangers inherent in such a stratagem. Why should the private sector (at which the pilot program and the subsequent legislation are primarily aimed) not take the Government's reckoning of the benefits at face value?

The *Discussion Paper*, in addressing the questions of 'what is in it and for whom', encapsulates the moving spirit of EEO. Listed first are the benefits to employers and organisations:

- better human resource management...[leading] to increased economic effectiveness.
- Affirmative Action Programs have been shown to reduce turnover and absenteeism by increasing individual employees' commitment to the organisation as they feel their skills are valued. The increase in job satisfaction means there is a consequent increase in productivity, which in turn increases the organisation's profitability.

- ...a positive public image of the organisation as a responsible and responsive employer. This encourages both men and women to apply for positions within the organisation. (1984:16)

Listed second are the benefits to employees:

- women and men will be able to exercise greater freedom of choice in respect of occupations from which they have previously been under-represented.
- a wider range of jobs should be opened up to women...
- new career structures should also open up to women employees...
- these factors should lead to an increase in job satisfaction. (1984:16−17)

Finally the benefits to unions:

- a breakdown in sex-based occupational segregation has to expand union membership...
- membership of unions will more accurately reflect the sex composition of the population...(1984:17)

And, more in the line of supporting argument — or reminder of undertakings given by the Australian Council of Trade Unions (ACTU) — there is an acknowledgment that women, especially married women, have been discriminated against in employment leading to the need to introduce structural changes to implement equal opportunity and affirmative acton programs (1984:17).

During 1984 we spoke to representatives of several of the major private sector employers who had volunteered to participate in the Pilot Program. They agreed to speak openly on condition that neither they nor their organisations be identified. As to why they had volunteered to participate in the Pilot Program several reasons were advanced:

- They had not actually volunteered: 'you get a letter from the Prime Minister asking if you'd like to participate in the Program and before you can reply you get a second letter thanking you for volunteering to participate';
- They were doing it already anyway in one corporate guise or another and not only with respect to women;
- It was part of being a good corporate citizen; but most importantly
- They saw what had happened in the United States, sensed the strengthening winds of legislative change in Australia and noted the increases in the rates of educational and workforce participation by women. They hoped that by participating in the program they

would be able to shape the legislation they felt would be an inevitable outcome, or that they would be granted some kind of
exemption from it, or that they might convince the government to
drop the whole idea of introducing legislation.

All of those to whom we spoke saw EEO/AA as the prerogative of
management and something which should be introduced in organ-
isationally specific ways. The Australian organisations were keen to
reject behaviour hitherto encouraged in their corporate cultures and
were ceasing to discriminate indirectly against women. The cream of
the female graduate crop was to be culled as energetically as the male
graduate crop; selection teams were being retrained to interview and
assess the 'company woman' as well as the 'company man'. Consultation about the Program appeared to be primarily between different
levels of management or, where the company was unionised, between
management and unions.

The major emphasis of the entire Pilot Program was fairly clearly
directed toward convincing employers, and to a lesser extent the
union movement, that they would be the major beneficiaries of the
legislation. While not all were convinced, the Government appears to
have been sufficiently successful in dampening the business community's overt hostility to the idea of legislation to warrant proceeding
with it.

The Pilot Program appears by and large to have treated women,
the intended beneficiaries, as a given. They are to become the taken-
for-granted objects of the legislation; their role in affirmative action
programs comes after the legislation has been enacted. The Commonwealth Affirmative Action (Equal Employment Opportunity for
Women) Act requires employers to consult with employees, especially
women employees, just as it requires employers to consult with trade
unions. But the requirement is for consultation, not participation,
and it is to occur after the rules of the game have been determined
elsewhere and the nature of the benefits to be bestowed decided by
others. It is worth recalling one staff survey conducted during the
Pilot Program which discovered 'many of its female staff are far more
interested in working at convenient hours and a convenient location
than in promotion opportunities' (Hope, 1986:66).

What is the nature of the benefit?

Equal Employment Opportunity programs concern paid legal employment. But exactly what opportunities are being offered by
employers to women, to ethnic minorities and in some instances to
Aborigines and to people with disabilites, and with whom are they to
be equal?

Once employed, individuals are to have the right to compete for some of the fruits of employment—promotion, leave and other entitlements—presumably also within the constraints of the availability of those fruits. Some, like equal pay for work of equal value, are forbidden. The key questions in all Equal Employment Opportunity and Affirmative Action programs are: opportunity equal to whom? and on whose terms? The answers which appear to have been given to date are: opportunities equal to those who already have them and on the terms set by those already in a position to determine them. As we have suggested elsewhere, one way to look at the import of the New South Wales Anti-Discrimination Act is to regard it as requiring that henceforth everybody is to be treated as if they were 'physically able, intellectually unimpaired Anglo-Celtic, heterosexual males'—provided they can pass. The frame of reference for Equal Employment Opportunity programs, the context in which they are to be implemented, makes their outcome inevitably limited.

One of the general benefits claimed for equal employment opportunity legislation is that it will put an end to the seniority system within the Public Service which disadvantaged women and recent arrivals to Australia. The criterion for advancement is to be merit. What merit means (other than that seniority is no longer to be the determinant) and how it can be measured in the context of employment have become contentious issues. Kalantzis, Issaris and Cope argue that

> The kinds of standards that are used to select on merit are indeed culture bound, but it is the culture of dominant, white, male, urbanised, industrialised, ethnics. Words such as 'resourcefulness', 'leadership', 'initiative' are used again and again in the Public Service Notices and job advertisements, all projecting a very accurate image of the person required rather than abilities or potential. It is of course possible, as has been done, to fit certain women and certain 'ethnics' into these same criteria, but this is simply a refinement of the pre-existing system. No real change has occurred which would alter the criteria selecting an elite group of 'anglo' and 'ethnic' males and females. The composition of the group may change, but the nature of it doesn't, nor does the structure which gave rise to it in the first place. Using the merit principle well, all middle class people are given equal opportunity for middle class jobs regardless of sex or ethnicity. (1985:14)

The solution thus far offered to difficulties of this type experienced by the intended beneficiaries of EEO programs has been to provide them with the opportunity to overcome what are construed as their deficiencies. The ubiquitous assertiveness training courses provided for women, ethnic minorities and now the physically disabled reinforce rather than contest the value attaching to such notions as leadership, initiative and assertiveness.

Anne Game, referring specifically to women, identifies another problem with such programs:

> ...there is a very clear subtext here that any failure can be attributed to women themselves, their inability to take up the opportunities. The 'catching-up' concept of equality is profoundly individualistic and lends itself to psychological and 'blame-the-victim' explanations for lack of success. (1984:254)

The opportunity, according to Game, that is being offered by the Commonwealth program for women is an opportunity for some women to do what is currently valued, that is, what men do. But what, she asks, of the women who do 'women's work'? (1985:256)

The other problem of course is that there are prerequisites for the employment opportunities being provided. For beneficiaries to enjoy equal opportunity in employment certain other 'benefits' must be made available, especially if those employment opportunities are to be conferred within the framework of equality with existing employment requirements and patterns. For women these include relief from child rearing responsibilities, and a fairer division of the domestic division of labour; for Aboriginal people the issues include health and housing; for migrants, language. Equal educational opportunity is a fundamental concern for all. These are matters at the heart of the processes which disadvantage members of these groups in the first place.

The question of pre- or corequisite benefits, by and large ignored, has been given some acknowledgment by the Commonwealth Government in the supportive measures it provides in certain directions. One of the areas best served is that of education where measures include a National Policy on Girl's Education, a Girls into Engineering Project, and Traineeships and Resource Agreements with states under which the states would collect data on the outcomes of girls' education. By way of further example, for all that so much remains to be done in the area of childcare, it has been recognised as critical in women's workforce participation, prompting Government intervention and a stout avowal of commitment in this field.

Who has benefited and in what ways?

There are two major problems involved in trying to gauge the success or otherwise of EEO legislation. The first revolves around competing claims for being 'the cause' of change, the second turns on the definition of what constitutes success and how much change must have occurred to be considered real or significant.

In large, complex societies it is not possible to attribute particular changes to specific pieces of legislation. Indeed, it is arguable that, given the massive shift in priorities required to include a reform on the political and then the legislative agenda, a particular piece of legislation is but a small indicator of the change that has already occurred. Women began moving into the workforce in large numbers long before the re-emergence of a large and active women's movement in the 1960s and 1970s and it was that movement's activities which led, among other things, to the enactment of EEO legislation in its various forms. On this line of argument, the legislation would not have been enacted until what it was designed to achieve had been partially accomplished already. What legislation does is reduce the legitimacy of the opposition to the changes already being wrought by other means. It lends moral authority to the push for change. The passage of legislation is an exercise in symbolic politics.

The second major difficulty lies in the fact that EEO/AA legislation was not enacted in isolation. In Australia, at roughly the same time, a series of government policies and programs were being introduced which either facilitated (in the sense of being corequisites) the implementation of EEO/AA legislation and/or which can lay equal claim to having been responsible for any changes that may have occurred. In the first category would have to go

- Freedom of Information legislation which, however weak, shifted the burden of justification from those seeking greater openness and access to information to those advocating the continuation of secrecy. It also provided better access to information about employment policies and practices which is essential in dealing with systemic discrimination.

- Occupational Health and Safety legislation which has enormous potential to be used in conjunction with EEO measures in addressing questions of workforce segregation. To be quite cynical, employers have begun to develop plans for career paths for women and to look at more flexible patterns of the organisation of women's work because RSI began to cost them money. They have also tried to deny the existence of RSI or, failing that, to deny their responsibility in causing it.

- Investigations into, and attempts to reform, the public services: for example, the Royal Commission on Australian Government Administration and the Review of New South Wales Government Administration. Indeed, the EEO amendments to the New South Wales Anti-Discrimination Act come out of that Review which was critical of inflexibilities in the organisation of work that prevent better use of the public service's human resources; better from the point of view of the particular department or authority and from the point of view of their employees.

- In New Wales the 1983 Public Finance and Audit Act which requires publicly funded organisations to be accountable for their use of those public funds on a much more broadly conceived notion of accountability than has hitherto been the case. Internal audit is no longer merely required to ensure that the financial books are balanced — it is concerned with the uses to which organisations put their resources, including their human resources.

- The Commonwealth Government's tentative moves to encourage industrial democracy and employer participation programs in both public and private sector organisations which it certainly regards as strongly linked both with Occupational Health and Safety and Affirmative Action legislation.

In the second category of programs and policies which can also lay claim to some of the credit for producing whatever changes that may have occurred in employment practices or statistics are those which cover the same groups as those covered by EEO legislation. If, for example, there have been changes in New South Wales in the numbers and patterns of employment of those people from minority ethnic backgrounds, are those changes due to EEO or the work of the Ethnic Affairs Commission or the general seepage into public consciousness of some notion of Australia as a multicultural society? Is it the range of government training and subsidisation schemes for Aborigines, and for encouraging the employment of women in technical and jobs other than traditionally female ones, that has led to any changes in employment patterns, or is it the EEO legislation?

One response to the question of what exactly is responsible for any changes that might have occurred is to argue that it doesn't really matter so long as the changes are occurring. A different response argues that it does matter, especially in a time of ever decreasing government expenditure on programs that are deemed to be 'wet'. If the slice of the government cake allocated to programs that try to remove the comparative disadvantage of particular groups in the community is diminishing irreversibly, effort and resources should go where they will be most effective. And the question must arise as to whether EEO legislation, as it has been implemented, has been and is the most effective means of achieving long-term redistributive outcomes for any or all of the groups it covers.

As well as the difficulty entailed in sorting out which programs can legitimately claim credit for which changes, there is the problem of agreeing on a definition of what will constitute success. How much change and of what kinds will have to occur and over what period of time before change can be deemed to have occurred? What givens, such as the 'state of the economy', are there? What means are there for sorting out changes which can be attributed to particular legislative measures or programs from changes which would probably have occurred in the long term anyway? What means are there for sorting out real changes from bureaucratic artefacts caused by the required form of reporting. For as we have demonstrated, to require organisations to list separately the number of new women appointees, the number of new Aboriginal appointees and the number of new appointees with physical disabilities can show, unwittingly, an increase in one of each when there may have been only one appointee — an Aboriginal woman with a physical disability. Nor can it be assumed that an intention to mislead is always absent. There are also, therefore, questions about the reliability of the data reported by which success or failure is measured and the checks it is possible to make on that data.

Changes claimed

In this section we look at the changes said to have been effected by the introduction of EEO legislation. The claims are seldom advanced by the intended beneficiaries.

New South Wales

The official source of information on the impact of the New South Wales Government's EEO legislation are the Annual Reports of the Office of the Director of Equal Opportunity in Public Employment (ODEOPE) presented to the New South Wales Parliament.

The Annual Reports provide an interesting insight into the priorities of the agency established by the legislation to perform its two major and somewhat incompatible functions. It must advise and assist the organisations covered by the legislation and it must judge or evaluate their performance in meeting the requirements of the legislation. The combination of functions makes it difficult for an organisation to disagree with the advice given or to decline a particular form of assistance offered. Indirectly, the agency is evaluating the quality of the advice and assistance it offers by one indicator—the degree of compliance with that advice and assistance.

All ODEOPE Annual Reports from 1981 to 1986 start with a tally of which organisations have submitted their EEO management plans and which have not, which plans were satisfactory to ODEOPE and which were not. A significant portion of the Annual Reports, particularly the early ones, was devoted to this, indicating the priority attached to the preparation of plans. There is a clear tendency toward bureaucratic goal displacement — where the means (plan preparation) to the ends of the legislation (change) become ends in themselves.

The next matter to receive attention in the Annual Reports was the status of the position of EEO Coordinator in the organisations covered; how many such positions had been created, whether they were full or part time, permanent or temporary, filled or vacant, occupied by women or men, and how many coordinators had attended what training programs.

Clearly some of the earliest people to benefit from the legislation were the occupants of EEO coordinator positions. Some observers saw the accelerated progression into and up from EEO coordinator positions by career public servants as equal employment opportunism. But what of the unfortunately named target groups? It is actually not so easy to tell who exactly has benefited from the legislation, in what ways or, a question that is not even addressed, at what cost to themselves. Claims of changes to employment patterns which are the result of the operation of the legislation are reported in such a way as to convey very little meaning. For example, most of the annual reports include a section on redistributive effects in the workforce; but what is provided is listings of raw numbers without the contextual statistical data needed for a reader to make sense of them, or other relevant information such as the state of the labour market or programs initiated from other sources aimed to improve the status and participation of women, Aborigines, migrants and people with physical disabilities.

Undoubtedly, part of the difficulty in deriving any meaningful appreciation of what is going on by reading the Annual Reports can be attributed to the quality of the information provided by the organisations required to report. The evidence is that statistical material is all too often paltry and inadequately analysed. This may be the result of ill-will, disobedience or lack of commitment to EEO. But it may be that organisations simply do not have that information readily available.

What, after nine years, has the EEO program in the New South Wales public sector achieved? According to Aller, there have been substantial gains. EEO did:

- provide a catalyst for the review and reform of inadequate personnel policy and practice;
- generate, for some organisations, the first systematic data on their employees;
- bring about discernible change in thinking within the public sector on discrimination and its impact;
- initiate significant education and staff development programs...
- generate a number of successful recruitment and promotion strategies to overcome underrepresentation of women and other target groups in occupation areas...

- provide an impetus for changes in restrictive selection such as the removal of unnecessary qualifications and some reduction in the use of seniority systems. (1989:24)

It would be hard to deny that the main beneficiary of these changes has been the public sector itself. Aller lists the limitations of the New South Wales program as the over emphasis on training and development at the expense of the removal of structural barriers; the over emphasis on getting numbers into promotional positions at the expense of improving the conditions of employment of the vast majority of the intended beneficiaries of the program who are stuck in positions with no career opportunities; an inadequate appreciation of the role of unions; and, given the ease with which some departments have dismantled their EEO units following a change of government, the failure to integrate EEO into organisations (1989:24–25).

Commonwealth Public Service

The Commonwealth Public Service Act requires all departments and some authorities to develop Equal Employment Opportunity programs for women and members of other designated groups. The first such programs were completed during 1985–86. Basically, the Commonwealth program follows the New South Wales model, which is not surprising given the overlap in personnel involved in their development. Similar sorts of arguments are advanced for the program and it has similar objectives.

The Public Service Board also conducted a Service-wide EEO survey in 1986, 'one of the most important studies of staffing within the Australian Public Service' (Public Service Board Annual Report, 1985–6:46), covering almost 200000 people. Conducted on the introduction of the EEO program, the intention was to 'update and extend this picture by extracting statistics from the personnel record systems...[which will] make it possible to monitor the results of EEO programs without conducting additional surveys' (1985–86:41). The intention was admirable because it avoided costly disruptive resurveys. But the Public Service Board was abolished on the recommendation of the 1987 Efficiency Scrutiny Unit and responsibility for EEO was devolved to departments. The Public Service Commission was created, with a small unit responsible for monitoring EEO programs. The 1987–88 *Annual Report of the Public Service Commissioner* provided some support for those who argued that the reorganisation of the Commonwealth Public Service would lead to a downgrading of EEO in the Service. Only 14 of the 25 agencies due to submit their first EEO programs between February and July 1988 had done so on time.

The *1987–88 Annual Report* was unable to make use of the 1986 benchmark Public Service Board Survey to provide comparative statistical information because of 'systems difficulties' (Jamieson, 1989:9). Moreover the *1988–89 Annual Report of the Public Service Commissioner* acknowledges little progress in this regard. An overall impression is that women have made some gains although these must be seen as qualified. Other sparse information on Aboriginal people indicates that they have not fared so well.

Within both the New South Wales and Commonwealth Public Services women appear to have been better able to take advantage of EEO programs than the other groups covered by them. Why this is so has not been seriously debated. It has been assumed that those responsible have simply not tried hard enough to enhance the employment prospects and statuses of the other groups. There is no recognition that the different target groups may begin the race up the organisational pyramid from different base lines. Nor is there any appreciation of the effects of the simultaneous targeting of several very different groups in a static labour market. Most important, and a theme to which we keep returning, is the assumption that the same legislative mechanisms can enhance simultaneously the employment status of women, Aborigines, ethnic minorities and people with physical disabilities, ignoring the very different processes that have disadvantaged, and continue to disadvantage, them. What works for (some) women cannot be assumed to work for Aborigines or other target groups. Inherent in the programs is a danger of 'feminising' the other groups to make them better fit the model that appears to be working for (some) women.

The private sector

Prior to the introduction of the Commonwealth Affirmative Action (Equal Employment Opportunity for women) Act in 1986 any private sector AA programs were voluntary. Some corporations, such as ESSO, had begun to move in this direction in the late 1970s. A Women in Management Program was introduced in August 1979. In that year ESSO developed an Anti-Discrimination Policy which became an EEO Policy in 1981 with further amendments being made to it in 1983. The policy follows the well-known rhetoric of equity, ultimately reducible to a credo of managerialism.

ESSO's public claims to success refer thus far only to women. Its approach to EEO is characterised by: a recognition that it is going to take a long time to make significant changes (at least a generation); a top down filter approach through the various levels of responsibility within the organisation(convince senior management first and it hits the shop floor five years later); divisional or departmental responsibility for developing specific EEO proposals and forward estimates in the context of the organisations overall five year plan annually adjusted; an insistence that EEO has to be organisation, even division, specific because of the particular corporate culture(s) of the organisation; a recognition of the need for research into the prospects for matching the corporation's present and future workforce needs with the current and future availability of skills and graduates; and an interpretation of EEO as a learning process primarily concerned with organisational (attitude and culture) change. ESSO's motivation for jumping the legislative gun was self-interest—they recognised the inevitability of legislation in Australia and they had done some homework on future human resources needs and which groups of the population would be likely to meet those needs.

The early results of the program were encouraging. In 1979, 3 per cent of the ESSO management/professional workforce were women but with an attrition rate of 50 per cent per annum. By 1985 this figure had risen to 11 per cent and the attrition rate had dropped to 10 per cent per annum, on a par with the male rate (Collins, 1989:3). Worldwide difficulties in the oil industry in 1986 affected ESSO badly. Staff were retrenched and recruitment ceased, and the women who had been recruited seemed to be having difficulty moving up the organisation. Some in ESSO saw the cause of this problem as the return of the high attrition rate among women and their solution was renewed recruitment efforts. Others tried to address some of the causes of the higher attrition rate by developing child care services, part-time work options and encouraging the return of professional women after maternity leave (Collins, 1989:4−5). ESSO's efforts seem to have reached a plateau. What will move it off that plateau appears, once again, to be self interest. It has done some more homework on its future human resources needs and who might meet them— 'women, non-caucasians and immigrants' (Collins, 1989:6): 'At ESSO, our EEO programme was initiated in response to demographic trends and it is a recognition of the implications of the recent demographic forecasts which will take us to the next level of achievement' (Collins, 1989:7).

The Commonwealth legislation which emerged out of the 1984 Affirmative Action Program in which ESSO and many others participated bears the marks of the influence of the private sector. It is facilitating legislation with weak sanctions for non-compliance with its reporting requirements.

The Affirmative Action Agency set up to implement the legislation has tabled three Annual Reports in Parliament: only the last two report on compliance. It is important to stress that: compliance with the legislation means compliance with its reporting requirements only. The Agency has no power to ensure compliance with the stated intent of the legislation—equal employment opportunity for women. In other words, only when an organisation, with no good reason, fails to send its report to the Agency, can it be subjected to the penalty provided for in the legislation—which is being named in Parliament.

The dwindling enthusiasm for EEO/AA evident in the New South Wales program and the Commonwealth Public Service appears to creep into private sector programs as well.

In 1989 Price Waterhouse Urwick (Management Consultants) invited 730 private sector Victorian companies to participate in a survey on issues surrounding the Commonwealth's Affirmative Action legislation. The survey was conducted, according to their Report 'as a service to the business community' (Price Waterhouse Urwick, 1989:4). While a cynic might regard the exercise as market research for the services of the organisation it is not entirely useless. In some ways the survey results reinforce some of the comments in the Affirmative Action Agency's *1988–89 Annual Report* which suggests some small reluctance in employer acceptance of the legislation. While only 157 companies responded to the questionnaire the summary findings are not surprising:

> the large majority of organisations do not find it difficult to comply with the minimum requirements of the Affirmative Action legislation. However, there is little evidence of organisations going beyond these requirements, and venturing into the more creative solutions to workforce issues such as job sharing and child care facilities...
> It is obvious that many organisations, whilst not experiencing any great difficulty with the logistics of the exercise, are yet to be convinced that the philosophical premise is valid...(1989:1–2)

One of the more interesting but not surprising findings was that the group most interested in affirmative action was management (for 41 per cent of respondents). The low level of interest evidenced by women employees covered by the survey is understandable given the benefits claimed and the beneficiaries named by the respondents. The main advantages nominated were:

- Enabling women to establish a career
- Increasing the pool of employees for management
- Providing a catalyst for systems review
- Improving staff morale
- Encouraging more people into under-represented trades
- Stabilising workforce (1989:36)

This, in 1989, is similar to the list of benefits the 1984 Pilot Program delivered to participating corporations.

Somewhat ironically, perhaps, the single major benefit common to all organisations covered by EEO legislation has been the light the reporting requirements has shed on the poor state of their personnel information systems.

While it is early times in assessing the impact of the Commonwealth legislation there is some echoing of the rhetoric the government used to sell it to the private sector — its major benefits will be to the private sector organisations it covers. Women seem increasingly unimpressed by its promise. A Silent Majority II Survey conducted in November 1988 asked a random sample of 1500 Australian homes (with a 68 per cent response rate) about their degree of concern for 187 problems. Although equal employment and promotion opportunities for women was listed as one of the 187 problems respondents could rank on the scale of degrees of concern, it did not make it into the top 40 areas of most concern. It was beaten into that list by, among others:

27 Stamp duty on house purchases too high
28 Servicing of new cars costs too much
30 Political advertising is mostly lies
34 Screening of same TV advertisement more than twice in hour
39 Politicians never keep their word. (Wright, *Sydney Morning Herald*:17.7.1989)

Bandwaggoners

There is another class of beneficiary which has emerged in a manner quite unforeseen. It comprises people who gain financially and in other ways distanced from the spirit of equality of opportunity by jumping on the bandwaggon of EEO. With eyes fixed on the new market they offer expensive, if not extensive, ranges of goods and services.

Since the early 1980s there has been a trail of seminars and workshops on presentation of self, personal power, assertiveness, communication and management. The market is principally women, usually women already on the road to success. They are, after all, the people for whom the messages might have meaning and who can afford to buy what is offered. Dressing for success and targeting the top are of little relevance to most Aboriginal people, migrants, people with disabilities or working class women, all of whom are likely to have a different set of priorities. It is true that some courses or workshops serving these groups have been offered through the agency of government, for example ODEOPE, but they are few and pale beside the hype of those offered to women. A good many of the presenters of these courses/workshops were once EEO/anti-discrimination workers employed within the public sector — but consulting is far more lucrative. One such person claims to be able to earn in three months' consulting what it used to take a year to earn working in the public service. They now sell to other women what they used once to offer in the name of sisterhood or out of the public purse in the name of public duty — their skills, their experience and their advice. Others are women who have visibly achieved in their own fields and who are then able to make a further success out of that achievement. But the message these successful women convey in seminars is not one of worker solidarity or even the mildest form of sisterhood. As Meredith Burgmann, who attended one session, wrote:

> The whole assumption of the conference was that feminism is about making it to the top. I questioned some of the women when it was over. All agreed that it had been a really worthwhile experience. They felt well informed and inspired.
> I asked if they felt inspired to help other women along the way. After some intelligent introspection they answered quite firmly that they did not. (*National Times*: 19.4.1984)

Established consulting firms were quick to offer new services to organisations faced with legislative requirements. They will provide assistance in designing affirmative action programs and in developing EEO in management. It is even possible to be issued with a certificate of attendance for management seminars and workshops; perhaps it is seen to suggest commitment.

Publishing has also prospered from EEO and the social climate promoting it. New magazines blazing the new message have appeared (and disappeared). The Editor's Note in the first issue of one magazine gives a very good idea of their style and their market:

> . . . designed and written specifically for the new breed of woman who wants information and strategies for professional and personal growth. . . Portfolio is not only for women in Business and the professions and those aspiring to join them, but also for homemakers who wish to keep informed and perhaps plan to return to a career. It is also for that army of women who support the welfare society with their voluntary work. The information in Portfolio is designed to help the woman who has a commitment to her work to address the problems and situations which are frequently of significance to women seeking their own identity and independence. . . (*Portfolio*, October/November 1984:1)

The re-emergence of the women's movement in the 1960s and 1970s and the development of women's studies programs and courses for post-secondary education has been a boon, above all, to book publishers. As bandwaggoners they have profited handsomely. Streams of titles and series have been produced — the women in the workforce, women in management titles are simply the icing on that already rich cake. Publishers have also benefited to a lesser degree from studies of migrants, ethnicity, racism and Aboriginal Australians: people with disabilities do not have that visibility yet.

Specific groups

Despite the inadequacy of official statistics there is evidence to suggest that EEO legislation (both here and in the US) has benefited only particular sections of some of the groups covered and in predictable ways. There is nothing inherently wrong with this. EEO legislation, by its nature, simply cannot live up to the expectations that the disadvantaged have had of it nor the dire consequences that its opponents fear from it. It is, at base, profoundly assimilationist.

Women

One of the indicators of which women have benefited from EEO legislation and the hype surrounding it is the sheer visibility of two groups of women. Firstly, the groups of women entering middle management and networking feverishly with each other; secondly, the lone pioneer intrepidly entering the world of traditional men's work — the first woman jockey, the first woman railway fettler, the first woman commercial airline pilot. Media coverage of the first group (at least the print media) is fairly constant. This is no doubt partly because of the suspicion that attaches to any formerly disadvantaged group which closes the gap between its members and the power brokers who determine the allocation of advantages. Of the second group, who are good visual media material, coverage is sporadic and peters out very quickly. After all, as Villiers (1986) points out, who is interested in the 'second woman to' or the 'fifteenth woman to'?

Women entering management are by far the most visible, the most studied and counted and their rising salaries the most sought after by advertisers. Consider the following titles:

'Women Learn to Play the Advertising Agency Power Game' (Claire Moffat, *The National Times*, 4–10 May 1984)
'Female Achievers in the Fast Lane' (Glennys Bell, *The Bulletin*, 10 September 1985)

'Beating Men at Their Own Game—How to Climb the
Corporate Ladder' (Ursula Woodhouse, *Sunday Telegraph*, 10
March 1986)
'Feminism and the Office—Strategies of Corporate Women'
(Barbara Ehrenlich, *The National Times*, 14—20 March 1986)
'How the Feminine Manager is Taking Over' (Hilary Gossage,
Daily Telegraph, 7 May 1986)
'Women are Making it Their Business to Succeed' (Liz Byrski,
The Australian, 17 June 1987)

Those who argue that women ought to be represented equally at all
levels of the organisation by simple value of an equal right to more
rewarding and influential positions will regard the movement of
women into middle management as slow but healthy. Those who
hope that 'organisations will be rendered humane, less oppressive,
and more conducive to genuine personal growth by the inclusion of
women' (Ferguson, 1984:121) are in for as big a disappointment as
those who believed that giving women the vote and allowing them to
stand for parliament would automatically have a civilising influence
on a brutish world. As Rhode points out:

> Individual rights-oriented stategies have succeeded largely in
> guaranteeing equal opportunities for advancement in male-defined
> structures under male-defined criteria. The principle beneficiaries
> have been females who are willing and able to conform to the male
> biography, those who accept the competitive, hierarchical
> structure of the workplace, together with the price the conformity
> extracts in the home...Those who succeed are those who
> acclimate to work environments structured by and for men.
> Through that process of acculturation, individuals tend inevitably
> to lose the incentive or perspective necessary to challenge the
> underlying structures and the purportedly neutral standards by
> which merit is assured. Thus the culture perpetuates itself,
> legitimized by the presence of a small percentage of women.
> (1986:155)

It is interesting to note that at the same time as women seem to be
reaching 'critical mass' in middle management, the language is becoming increasingly masculine, borrowing from competitive sport, the
military and according to Hearn and Parkin (1987:147—148), with
terms like 'policy thrusts', 'projections' and 'market penetration', from
the language of masculine sexuality. Everything has to be managed—
time, people, stress, performance and image; everyone is an achiever—
fast, over, under or quiet. We have high fliers and fast trackers, we
have people targeting the top and EEO legislation targeting disadvantaged groups; the 1960s woman feared success, the 1980s
woman dressed for it; we have people who lead effectively, com-
municate assertively and thrash ideas out. Corporations have missions,

plans, goals and objectives. Passive sounding nouns are changed into active sounding verbs like mentoring, prioritising or networking. And we have strategies as well as strategic thinking, strategic planning, strategic decision making. If managers could admit to acting defensively from time to time, with strategic initiatives they could bring Star Wars into the boardroom.

The move into management is full of contradictions for women. Ferguson argues that 'advice to upwardly mobile women directs them to retain the form of feminine interactional skills but to abandon the content' (1984:94).

Ethnic minorities

Which among the ethnic minorities has benefited from EEO legislation and what has been the nature of that benefit? For this targeted group it is virtually impossible to disentangle which policy initiative led to what. Indeed, there is considerable competition for credit. Unionists, for example, are keen to point out that English language classes on the job were a union, not an EEO, initiative. EEO legislation, enacted when it was, has largely reinforced the pattern of benefit-bestowing already started by multicultural initiatives. The beneficiaries are primarily the middle class ethnic elites; the benefit, participation in the dominant political culture at a level which, while it does not give direct access to broadly based power, does give access to the power of the broker—translating, for a commission, what those below them want into the currency of what those above them will give.

Government reports, apart from chastising organisations for not achieving as much for ethnic minorities as they have for women, convey a very blurred picture of the impact of EEO legislation on the group they are most interested in, those from Non-English-Speaking-Backgrounds. In most reports, as Kalantzis, Issaris and Cope (1985) point out, the 'children of migrants who for the greater part of their childhood have been educated and raised in Australia' are categorised as of Non-English-Speaking-Backgrounds, together with those who migrate as adults. The conflation does not mask problems, it generates them.

Even a broad distinction between Australian and overseas-born people whose first language is not English is not so helpful—how much difference is there between being born overseas and migrating at the age of one and being born in Australia? Far greater differences are likely between those born overseas and migrating at one, fifteen, thirty and sixty, but these are not addressed. Similarly, EEO, like multiculturalism (Jupp: 1986) by and large ignores country of origin—placing together Greeks and Italians with Lebanese, Turks and Vietnamese.

One of the two major emphases of EEO for non-anglophone ethnic minorities is on recognition of professional qualifications obtained overseas. While warranting some attention, it is important to recognise how small a group of migrants this emphasis benefits and just who they are—predominantly male and middle class and obviously educated. It enables the class and gender divisions in countries of origin to be faithfully reproduced within ethnic communities in their country of adoption. The other major emphasis of EEO, which it borrowed (certainly in New South Wales from the Ethnic Affairs Commission), is on 'identified positions'. While this may offer some form of reserved employment it runs the risk of locking individuals into particular positions and of locking particular ethnic groups into particular types of employment. To identify positions for Turks or Lebanese, for example, can easily be turned around to argue that Turks and Lebanese are good only in those positions.

The shift in official policy from assimilation to integration of migrants in the mid 1960s and thence to multiculturalism in the 1970s differs only in sophistication, rhetoric and the identity of those setting the terms and conditions for immigrant participation in 'the good life' (see, for example, Jakubowicz, 1981; Jakubowicz, Morrissey and Palser, 1984; Seitz and Foster, 1985; Carsariga, 1986). Now the brokers are the new ethnic middle class for whom, as Jakubowicz points out, 'the entire ethnic relations industry was created' (1985:274). And EEO has wholeheartedly plugged itself into multiculturalism. It does not distinguish between countries of origin, let alone regions or class position within countries of origin, nor whether migrants arrived as part of a skills recruitment drive, as political refugees or under family reunion schemes. Nor does it take account of age at immigration or of migration. All of these factors are identified as crucial in labour market studies of immigration.(See, for example, Chapman, 1986; Collins, 1984; Mistilis, 1985; Sloan and Kriegler, 1984; Strombach, 1986.) By its very nature EEO legislation simply cannot address the basic disadvantaging process for non-anglophone ethnic minorities.

Aborigines

There is potent irony attached to EEO legislation which requires the same special efforts for both immigrants and Aborigines (for whom other Australians are all immigrants) who are treated as ethnic minorities in their country of origin. It is not the act of migration which disadvantages Aborigines but the long and continuing process of being dispossessed in and of their own land and colonised. It is unlikely that, alone, EEO legislation would be able to claim very many successes for Aborigines.

It is unrealistic to expect EEO legislation to enhance the position of Aborigines in white Australia in the short term. Exhortations to 'try harder' simply increase the pressure on the minority of the Aboriginal community who have reached the threshold of being potential beneficiaries of the legislation. As Barlow comments, Aborigines everywhere are pressured to become more like white Australians which '...would make it easier for administrators, service organisations, entrepreneurs and governments to negotiate with them...' (1984: 104—105). Barlow lists policies imposed on Aborigines in the last twenty years alone, each requiring change: assimilation, integration, self-management, and to that list must be added being the target of EEO legislation.

There are far too many prerequisites to being able to benefit from EEO legislation which simply have not yet been met. The first is sheer survival. The infant mortality rate for Aboriginal Australians is 26.2 per 1000 live births (with state and territory variations) compared with 10.0 per 1000 for non-Aboriginal Australians (Department of Aboriginal Affairs, 1984:115). Aboriginal life expectancy at birth is about 20 years less than that for non-Aboriginal Australians.

Despite the fact that education is compulsory for all Australians, at the 1981 Census 3.6 per cent of Aborigines had left school before they reached 13 years of age and 10 per cent had never attended school at all. For non-Aboriginal Australians the figures are 2.8 per cent and 0.8 per cent respectively. For those Aboriginal children who do stay on at school the difficulties increase for them and their families. With the median annual family income for Aborigines at 55.1 per cent of that for non-Aboriginal Australians, the low retention rate for Aborigines is understandable. At the 1985 New South Wales Higher School Certificate, the retention rate for Aborigines was 6.9 per cent compared with 36.13 per cent for the non-Aboriginal community but even then, 75 per cent of the Aboriginal students who sat the examinations were placed in the bottom 25 per cent of the state. But as Bob Morgan, President of the New South Wales Aboriginal Educational Consultative Group, commented, 'the mere fact that the Aboriginal students survived in a system that is culturally weighted against them is an achievement in itself' (Burney, 1986:10).

Figures from the 1986 Census indicate little improvement. While 60 per cent (67 per cent of women and 54 per cent of men) of the Australian population (15 years and over) have no qualifications 75 per cent (77 per cent of women and 74 per cent of men) of the Aboriginal population have no qualifications. Yet only 6 per cent (5 per cent of women and 7 per cent of men) of the Australian population was unemployed while 17 per cent (12 per cent of women and 23 per cent of men) of Aboriginal Australians were unemployed (ABS 1986 Census, Tables CA0057, CA0052 and C21, C25 of Small Area

Data, Format CSC.07). Sykes points out that the private sector has been disgracefully and unconscionably slow in employing blacks (1989:79).

This is not to suggest that Aborigines should be denied employment opportunity but to argue that the approach which implies that the paucity of Aborigines in the New South Wales public sector can be attributed to 'insufficient determination' on the part of departments and authorities grossly oversimplifies the disadvantages of being Aboriginal in non-Aboriginal Australia. It also preempts debate over the fundamental question of the legitimacy of the intended beneficiaries of any piece of legislation determining their benefits. The peccable records of Australian governments in response to the Aboriginal quest for land rights clearly indicates the very severe limits that those who are in a position to bestow benefits place on the participation of beneficiaries.

People with physical disabilities

People with physical disabilities are the group most recently targeted to receive the benefits of EEO legislation (1984 in New South Wales). And they are quite inappropriately included in the grab-bag of disadvantage. We would presumably prefer to do away with physical disability in a way that we would not wish to do away with Aboriginality, ethnicity or gender. At best we could, with a different set of priorities, reduce the incidence of physical disability in the population through improved access to better medical services and through safer workplaces and work practices. The need to address the processes that disadvantage each of the groups covered by EEO legislation stands out most starkly with people with physical disabilities. Would it not, for example, be a more significant achievement for the public sector to stop disabling its own workforce than to appoint and promote a target number for the employment of people with disabilities?

Table 5.1 Causes of death

Cause of death	Number per Annum
Medical misadventure (a)	56
Homicide (b)	319
Industrial/work related death (a)	579
Suicide (b)	2240
Motor vehicle traffic accident (b)	2783

Source: (a) Average 1982–1984 (Harrison, Frommer, Ruck and Blyth, 1989)
　　　　(b) 1987 Australian Bureau of Statistics

A selection of some of the causes of death in Australia is revealing in terms of the hazards of paid employment (see Table 5.1). Given the focus of this discussion it is important to note that in New South Wales over the period 1985−86, for every workplace fatality that was compensated there were more than 500 work injuries that were not fatal but which resulted in time off work plus compensation (Harrison, Frommer, Ruck and Blyth, 1989). And one third of all compensable workplace injuries are attributable to manual handling (National Occupational Health and Safety Commission, 1987:1).

Australia does not appear to have a very good record on industrial injuries: in fact, no official record appears at all. The ILO *Year Book of Labour Statistics* which provides annual statistics on occupational injuries, fatalities and workdays lost through injuries has figures for most African, European and American countries and for Asia and Oceania, but no figures for Australia. The Australian Commonwealth *Year Books* have no figures and refer readers to state collections of statistics.

There are other important differences between legislating for EEO for people with disabilities and others. As Nothdurft and Astor remind us, there has not been a liberation movement behind the move of the physically disabled into the public policy and social legislation arena. Nor is there the same body of literature that is widely available for the other groups. And while we disagree with the latter part of their claim that 'People with disabilities are not a homogeneous group in the way that, say, women or Aborigines may be for the purposes of interviewing' (1986:346) (since neither women nor Aborigines nor ethnic minorities constitute homogeneous groups), their main point, that there are vast differences between the experiences and needs of people with different disabilities, certainly stands. The employment and other life prospects of people with disabilities will also vary depending upon the age at which they were disabled. To have been blind from birth presents challenges of an order different from those confronting persons blinded after school and even university education have enabled them to attain desirable employment qualifications. Nor are people with physical disabilities undifferentiated by sex, class or ethnic background.

It is all the more unfortunate that for EEO purposes there has been a homogenising approach to physical disability. Both the Commonwealth and the New South Wales programs require self-definition. Without wanting to construct hierarchies, to join those who simply have to wear spectacles (mild/moderate even severe sight defect) with those who are totally blind or confined to a wheelchair blows the plight of the bespectacled public servant out of all perspective.

At what cost to the beneficiaries?

It should not surprise us that the primary beneficiaries of EEO programs thus far have been the middle class elites of the groups covered, primarily women and to a lesser extent men with minority ethnic backgrounds. EEO has simply helped them assimilate into the mainstream because they were already at least halfway there. They shared the values of the mainstream and in a sense were merely fighting to be recognised and rewarded for reinforcing the view that those values are the correct and proper ones for a society like ours. Once accepted there is no attempt to alter the basic distribution of resources in the system that has so honoured them. They in turn become the brokers for successive waves of would-be entrants, teaching them the rules by which the game must be played.

Yet this mobility is not achieved without cost both to the individuals on the move and to the communities from which they come. There is a considerable volume of material on the superwoman/supermum syndrome — the woman who not only makes it in the public sphere but is a high achiever in other senses. The cost to some femocrats is alienation and isolation from the movement which gave them the strength and the reason to move into the the public service arena. There is also some evidence to indicate that Aborigines pay for the privilege of advancement in public sector employment (Lovejoy and Cummings, 1989).

We know less of the cost of Affirmative Action/EEO programs borne by the communities from which targeted individuals are plucked. Bonacich writes:

> Who is helped by affirmative action? Does it help the communities from which people are brought forth? Or does it help the dominant order? I would contend the latter...First, it improves the public statistics on the distribution of people across social strata so that those at the bottom can no longer base their sense of oppression on racism or sexism. They are now even more forced to blame the victim — themselves...Second, it reinforces the dominant ideology of individualism. Social benefit, it says, is achieved through individual advancement...
>
> Third...affirmative action strips communities of their intelligentsia. Those people who might have become leaders and thinkers on behalf of their people, who might have dared to raise the dangerous questions of our time, are plucked off and brought in and domesticated and thereby silenced.
>
> Finally, these new recruits to the professional-managerial stratum are themselves made into watchdogs of their communities...With a vested interest in social stability because of

their new-found status and wealth, the minority and female middle class now tries to appease the class struggle. They play a vital role in stabilizing the class struggle. (1987:108−109)

6

Babies and bathwater

Being some concluding remarks about the processes whereby women, Aborigines, migrants and people with physical disabilities are disadvantaged and about the limitations of EEO in dealing with those disadvantaging processes.

Time has wrought changes in our view of EEO, which has fulfilled neither the hopes nor the fears of its early characterisation. Some members of the groups covered have profited from it. For the majority there have been few changes. Fundamenally their social position and even conditions and opportunities in employment remain much as they were. By the same token, the dire consequences prophesied to follow the introduction of EEO have not come to pass. The Australian way of life has not crumbled, its values remain intact, the family persists and there is no evidence to suggest that standards in the workplace have fallen. What has become clearer is that the various pieces of EEO legislation and EEO programs, although significant in themselves, cannot achieve equality in employment, nor even equality of opportunity in employment, for their subject groups. Their significance lies heavily in the attention they focus on existing inequalities and inequities. Advertently or not the successes and failures of EEO, sometimes simply its existence, draw attention to and highlight aspects of social participation and dimensions of inequality hitherto of little concern. It is also true that EEO is greatly enhanced by steps taken to address matters such as extending the provision of child care facilities, introducing educational access programs and English language classes. Yet, ironically, one of the flaws in the working of EEO has been a failure to appreciate the dynamic complexity of the problems facing various disadvantaged social groups. Central to this dynamic are questions of attitude, interests and values and the power to advance and uphold them.

It is evident that we can learn a great deal from existing legislation, and indeed that we should. There is a question, however, which continues to niggle. Is this what we, the subject groups, want? Perhaps we should ask more sharply: is this all we want? If we are not careful we may get little more.

The introduction of EEO legislation was a political and highly visible response by legislators to voices calling for reform. But because something was done, or perhaps was seen to be done, danger lies in the assumption that nothing more need be done. Whatever surgery might be performed on the current EEO legislation, it will remain inadequate if what we seek to achieve is fundamental, widespread and enduring change in patterns of participation in employment, thereby opening the way for previously disadvantaged groups. Since the relationships of work cannot usefully be conceived as separate from other social relationships, this then means changes in social structures, not simply changes within the existing arrangements which both reflect and reinforce those structures. But this fundamental renegotiation of relationships was never the intention, indeed the intention appears to have been to postpone such change (indefinitely, if possible) by distributing distracting baubles.

So long as EEO is principally concerned with the outcomes of employment discrimination, or at best the iceberg tip of discriminatory practices, it inhibits its own effectiveness. We ought to be taking serious account of the reasons which render some groups vulnerable to discriminatory practices in employment. The enquiry must grapple with the question of identifying the disadvantaging processes whereby women, Aborigines, migrants and people with disabilities are seen as 'other' and marginalised in relationships rated high on a scale of social significance and rewarded accordingly. What follows is some discussion of disadvantaging processes.

For women

Over the centuries many women, and sometimes men, have deplored, even railed against, the socially unequal position of women. The inequality of women is manifest in circumscribed opportunities to participate in society across a range of valued activities, whether political, intellectual, artistic, scientific or whatever. It is evident in their subordination (even within their allotted domain — the private) and in the qualification of their property rights in their persons. Those who struggled against these strictures often enough suffered the appropriation of their work or the devaluation or neglect of their contribution and themselves as contributors (see Spender, 1982).

The point is that there is nothing new in the subordination of women. Although the quest for origins is fruitless, giving rise to sometimes absurd, at other times specious, and at all times unsubstantiable speculation (whether Bachofen's *Mutterrecht* or sociobiologistic accounts), we can see well enough the processes constituting that subordination. They are cultural processes which operate, in one

form or another, across societies and through time. While there is
variation between societies and over time in the particular manifestations of that oppression there is a common and constant element
in that women's location is seen, first and foremost, in the domestic
sphere. This seems to be one of the strongest reasons prompting
biologistic approaches to women's social subjugation. Their do-
mestication leads fairly directly to naturalising arguments premised
on women as child bearers. Women's proper location in 'the natural
private sphere of the family' has been legitimated in being advanced
by notable male philosophers and political commentators (see
Pateman's discussion of Hegel's theory, 1988:176−7), but it has been
promoted by all manner of persons regardless of the measure of
attention they have given to the subject. Prior to this, and indeed in
most silences on the mater, we may guess it generally to be assumed.

The following points cover well-worn ground but bear restating.
Women's biological ability to bear children, not shared by men although, interestingly enough, culturally arrogated by men in certain
circumstances (see Hiatt, 1971), has been very loosely translated into
the responsibility to care for them. Somehow linked to all this is a
whole series of myths, or at least cultural constructions, of the essential
characteristics of women. This cultural overlay transforms sexual
difference into political difference in which the subject becomes not
women but Woman. The category Woman, writes Pateman (1988:17)
is regarded as natural and timeless, 'defined by certain innate, biological characteristics'. But it is, she warns, 'a figment of the patriarchal imagination'.

Women can (and should, it is said) do many things. Apart from
bearing and caring for children, although in some senses clearly
related, women nurture and care for the old, the ill, the needy. Their
work is loving and caring, but very importantly it is also servicing:
they service men at home and in the workplace. They have the
capacity, and again hence the responsibility, to make a house a home.
There is a swag of other attributes gratuitously conferred on women,
engraving the stereotype in high relief: they can perform fiddly tasks,
they exercise patience, they are compliant — and so the list continues.
Men can and should do many things too. The difference is that
women's talents and responsibilities are framed negatively — they are
deemed to prevent women from being able to do other things which
men can and should, such as exercise authority, think linearly, participate in public life. The reverse does not hold. That is, men can
cook, sew, look after children, be demonstrably affectionate, but they
do not see it as appropriate and choose, or are pressured, not to (see
Poiner, 1990).

The division and separation of the private from the public realm is a fundamental feature of the process of disadvantaging women. The division, undeniable in everyday practice, is underscored and invested with further meaning in the way it is conceptualised and theorised. Pateman argues that the private sphere is acknowledged as the proper and necessary foundation for public life, yet it is viewed as inconsequential in political theory and political activism. Women, while naturalised, are not left behind in a state of nature but incorporated as quiescent passive beings into the private realm, the silent partner in the social order (Pateman, 1988:11). Indeed, the paradoxical and contradictory nature of women's incorporation into civil society has eluded many. Pateman continues: had women been clearly excluded from civil life there would have been no questioning the problem, but they have been incorporated in a way which apparently guarantees their freedom. Yet simply because of their sex, which defines them as 'out' or 'other' or at least as secondary in social arrangements established by and on behalf of men, women's freedom is circumscribed (1988:222−34). Times may be a-changing, but ever so slowly and with much backsliding. For all the rhetoric, many of the policies and some of the programs, most women remain subordinate in the public and the private sphere. So long as women who work in the private sphere are not given, and seen to be not given, social autonomy and social power, and whilever the work they perform there goes unrecognised and unrewarded (see Waring, 1988) it is difficult to see how women's (not one or two, but generally) participation in the public sector can be qualitatively, quantitatively and enduringly improved.

De Lepervanche points out that the significance of women in the public arena in Australia has stemmed from their family position as 'breeders' and as guardians of morals (de Lepervanche, 1989a, 1989b; see also Summers, 1975). Bear in mind though, their significance has been as breeders of little white Australians and guardians of Anglo-Celtic values enshrined within the developing Australian tradition (de Lepervanche, 1989a, 1989b), in itself characteristically masculine. Women have not usually acted autonomously in these matters but rather in response to pressures from the (male) social order, often enough from the state. The process has confirmed the centrality of the family and their socially secondary position. Continuing debates on the issue of abortion underscore the role of women as breeders, although contradictions steeped in racism surround the use of Depo Provera on Aboriginal schoolgirls against their will (de Lepervanche, 1989a:51).

At this point it is challenging to ask the question: Does EEO give primacy to paid work over private life and thereby unintentionally devalue not only the private sphere but, given their place in it, women? The strange consequence of this, of course, is for EEO to underwrite its own limitations. The process is more comprehensible when we take into account that being in the public domain, programs initiated by the state will be constituted by masculine values and interests.

For all that the position of women in the family is critical in their general social subordination, the family is not an isolated institution in the social process. Rather there is continuing interplay between the family and other social forms. The relations of gender, so clearly defined in the domestic setting, are central in the delineation of women's workplace relations which, and at the same time, constitute gender relations in the family (Cockburn, 1983; Walby, 1986; Franzway, Court and Connell, 1989). The issue is not simply women's numbers in the workforce, it is the type of work they do and the levels of employment in which they are found. In Australia they have long been in paid employment, but in secondary positions. As de Lepervanche points out, by 1910 one-fifth of the workforce was female (1989b:43) but these women were heavily concentrated in areas seen as women's work, carrying less prestige and lower wages than men's work. Australia continues to have very marked occupational segregation by sex; the undervaluing of women's work and women's skills has direct consequences for the continuing gap between female and male wages despite the 1972 Equal Pay legislation. It is true that there is some breaking down of the sexual segregation of the workforce and there have been many state-initiated programs to attract women to non-traditional occupations. But the truth is that the benchmarks for success in employment are masculine. Pateman's words, 'that women's equal standing must be accepted as an expression of the freedom of women *as women* and not treated as an indication that women can be just like men' (1988:231), are salutary here. It is not only that women are seen as different from men, for men are also different from women (although that generates a different response) (see Lloyd, 1989:16), it is that the masculine in thinking and attitudes, in behaviour, in social structures and relationships, is taken as the norm. It is not a big hike for sexual difference to be perceived and expressed as political difference.

The constitutive processes which disadvantage women work through the designation of women as domestic; and through the masculine structures and relations of the workplace, they also work through a complex of other interactive relationships. Women's education differs from men's in length, content and even in its style. Men tend to be educated longer and are oriented to different fields of study and qualifications. The real question is education to what ends? Given their 'primary and proper' location, such interrogation has always been vexed for women, although the plaudits given to 'cultured' women (or were they given to their husbands?) opened educational avenues for some, notably the class privileged. Now, given slavish support for education through training in applied fields of science, technology and economics, those subject areas which were previously open and welcoming to women at secondary and tertiary levels of education are losing economic and hence popular support and status. If women want to exercise power in the public sphere or even want to participate with credibility, there is increasing pressure on them to look like men.

As Burton discusses (1985:114−129), the education system is one dimension of state intervention in the reproduction of relations of production and it is, as she says, very powerful. The state's connections with gender relations, however, which go well beyond the educational system, are both contradictory and paradoxical. Of recent years there has been a range of policies and programs introduced by state and Commonweath governments specifically directed, it is claimed, to benefit women. The problem here, as Pateman points out, is that 'the power and capriciousness of husbands is being replaced by the arbitrariness, bureaucracy and power of the state, the very state that has upheld patriarchal power' (1989:200). As she argues, to make women directly dependent on the state (a consequence of many interventionist policies) will not by itself challenge patriarchal power relations, although the increasing public visibility and voice of women may give some leverage. There is also a contradiction in the emphasis, which is unwaning, that the state gives to the centrality of the family in Australian life. The ideology of the family, for all that it is less frequently expressed in its traditional form, provides the rationale for policies which lock women into providing private welfare. It also reinforces the identity of women as dependent on men who, as the principal breadwinners, enjoy dominance in private and public spheres, and it affords men tax relief while exacerbating the likelihood of poverty among women (see Burton, 1985:104−111; Pateman, 1989:185−204).

EEO, as one dimension of state intervention to improve women's position in society, has had a mixed reception. The publication of submissions on Equal Opportunity and Equal Status for Australian Women, invited by the House of Representatives' Standing Committee on Legal and Constitutional Affairs, attests the range of responses. While some assert its success, others denounce its failure. Generally, however, the views are that EEO is a good idea but that it is not working well or, more optimistically, that is is not working well yet. Some who claim it as a good idea argue that at best it can have but limited effectiveness. The cautions and caveats relate directly to the multidimensional nature of disadvantage and indirectly its interactive characteristics.

For Aboriginal people

Writing fifteen years ago, Rowley argued that Aborigines had special group needs related to the penalties they had suffered in white-dominated Australia. He also stressed that policies intended to change social relationships but which were aimed at individuals and which ignored the broader social context and history of these relationships can have but limited succcess (1972b:416–7).

The relationship of Aboriginal people with white Australian society was modelled in the circumstances of conquest and settlement. Over the years there have been social changes wrought in both Black and white societies. Yet, the essential pattern of race relations has remained the same and whites have continued to colonise Aboriginal people, conceptually and in very material ways. Rowley observed that white Australians are greatly attracted by the notion of 'inevitable progress' (1972b:430; 1972c:358), which is towards an ideal state defined by dominant sectors of the dominant society and, unsurprisingly, mirroring their interests and values. An obvious problem is that this idea of progress has nonetheless retained social differentials, and the danger is that even as the lot of Aboriginal people improves, the distance between Aboriginal and other Australians does not apparently decrease. Certainly some Aborigines have through their own struggles made significant achievements in white Australia but, referring again to Rowley, gains for individuals or even communities do not bring Aboriginal society generally into equal participation.

In the last couple of decades, and with very few exceptions, the style of enquiry into what might loosely be described as race relations in Australia was in itself a barrier to understanding. Precious little has been written on Aboriginal history (Biskup, 1982; Reynolds, 1981); Australian historiography has been concerned with white Australia. So long as Aborigines were written out of history there was no need to raise the question of race relations; such a question only really emerges in visibly problematical contexts.

Excised from Australian history, Aborigines were nonetheless to become the subject group of Australian research. This work was undertaken by whites but focused nearly exclusively on Aborigines (cf. white relations with Aborigines) and has lead to Black culture being branded as the factor limiting the effectiveness of Aboriginal people as social participants in white Australian society (see Rowley, 1972b:182).

Certainly the idea that Australia was colonised, that is to say founded, not conquered, had disadvantaged Aborigines from the earliest times of white settlement. As soon as the armchair vision of noble savage faded and the policy of 'amity and trust' crumbled (see

Stanner, 1968:7) Aborigines were characterised as beyond the pale of society. Either by the formulation of policy or in some cases the failure to formulate it, Aboriginal people were made non-significant ('other') in economic, legal and political terms.

Following the white invasion Aboriginal populations decreased rapidly. The carnage of tribal wars is little recognised. Starvation following the appropriation of their lands and the clearance of native fauna and flora also took a dreadful toll, as did the introduction of diseases. These were features of a laissez-faire extermination (see Smith, 1980:6). But extermination had another and appallingly active dimension, and many Aboriginal people were, in one form or another, wilfully murdered by the Europeans.

When labour was in short supply, a theme of Australia's history, Aborigines were recruited. Those who refused to 'cooperate' or who even actively resisted the white invasion of their land became targets of settler anger. Aborigines may have been pronounced British subjects but they did not derive benefits from the British system of law. The pattern of prosecutions on the unpeaceful frontier was monotonously the same; Aborigines were invariably deemed to be the offenders and suffered the inevitable punishment — expropriation of their land and often death. Whites triumphed and were rewarded with that same land (Rowley, 1972a:153; Sykes, 1989:84).

The fall from grace from the Rousseauian ideal was closely tied to the threat to white economic interests which Aborigines were seen increasingly to offer. When they sought to retain associations with their land, and particularly when they hunted introduced animals grazing on it, Aborigines were swiftly reclassified as nuisances, even vermin. If they retaliated against the various forms of violence dealt them by the Europeans, they were vilified further. The basis for the attitudes of ensuing generations, Black and white, was laid in the conditions of conquest and maintained in the historical view of those relationships.

It is a legacy which has rebounded on Aborigines time and again. For instance, the failure of Aboriginal claims in the Gove land case was attributed by Stanner to this distortion of history.

> If there is one thing more clear to me about the Yirrkala case than anything else it is the paradox that if the Aborigines had by accident or design pleaded and established the truth — that Australia was a conquered and not a settled colony — and thereby committed legal suicide, they could not have fared worse than by falling in, under legal advice, with the untruth that it was a settled colony. Under the law applying to a conquered people the British Crown by prerogative act could have lawfully extinguished all their rights. According to the Blackburn judgement, it did the

same lawfully under the law applying to settled colonies. The
conclusion is inescapable. The Aborigines by law were held to be
outside the category of human beings, though British subjects.
(Cited in Barwick, Beckett, and Reay, 1985:40)

Over the years there have been pronouncements of the demise of
the Aboriginal population and of Aboriginal society. But even as
Blacks were dying from starvation, disease and white brutality, the
number of children born of mixed unions increased. The overwhelm-
ing majority of these children were raised by their mothers in Aboriginal society. Since estimates of the Aboriginal population did not
take account of people of mixed descent, the figures — at best very
questionable — were hopelessly out. After decades of ludicrous classification premised on 'the degree of blood' (for example, half-castes,
quadroons, even octoroons), the significance of identification on the
basis of social association was recognised. Since 1971 information has
been collected on the basis of self-identification, that is, people of
Aboriginal descent identify as Aboriginal or not, as they choose. At
the 1986 census 227 645 people, that is 1.5 per cent of the Australian
population, registered as Aboriginal or Torres Strait Islander. The
myth of a dying race must be seen in the light of wish projection on
the part of members of the white population. Moreover, the persistence
of Aboriginal assertions of cultural differences, the vigour with which
they are made, and a clear desire to be counted Aboriginal, suggest a
rejection of domination, white attitudes and views. The claims place
value on Aboriginal attitudes, beliefs and practices, rejecting imput-
ations of inferiority.

The idea that Aborigines were dying out encouraged a general
attitude of indifference to their relations with an increasingly white
Australia. At best Europeans were concerned to 'smooth the pillow of
a dying race' and for many decades it was a matter of out of sight, out
of mind. Following this principle, and quite in conformity with the
social Darwinism underlying an expectation that Aboriginal society
would be extinguished, was the development of measures to 'protect'
surviving Aborigines. Relief, it was argued, could best be extended to
them in a careful and regulated way when they were gathered
on reserves and missions. Thus Aborigines were institutionally marginalised. One disturbing aspect of such protection was the erosion of
language and cultural ties, and the usurpation of initiative. Moreover
the reserves, which many Blacks have since dubbed concentration
camps, often acted as pools of labour which ensured that insofar as
Aborigines were incorporated into white society, it was as an under-
class of labour. The legacy of these early relations remains and the
question today is how much real change has there been to the traditional models of Aboriginal women as domestic servants and Ab-

original men as labourers, and Aboriginal people generally as no-hopers and bludgers.

When administrative policy formally shifted towards the assimilation of Aborigines into white Australian society, a scarring structural assymetry was written into the process. It is clear that at the time of the formulation of a doctrine of assimilation most proponents had a rose-tinted view of it. The belief, as enunciated, was that the social incorporation of Aborigines would bring about equality of opportunity—that is, that Aborigines had the same needs and hopes as white Australians and given the same access to, say, education and employment would derive benefits of the same order as whites. Most Aboriginal people resisted this view strongly. Criticism focused mainly on the fact that assimilation required Aborigines to relinquish cultural differences and to be mute, indeed to disappear, as a separate group with a separate identity. The imperative of assimilation was identified as 'become, not just of us but like us'.

In the sixties there was a change in white Australian attitudes; Blacks were no longer forced into ceding their identity according to assimilationist principles. Previous beliefs that they should be ignored, protected, civilised or rendered invisible lost currency. As well, historians began to break their oppressive silence. Most importantly, it is only since then that the voices of Aborigines have been heard at all over those of whites, whether critics or mentors. In 1967 a referendum was held changing the Constitution to give Aboriginal people Australian citizen's rights. Bandler points out the referendum stimulated a greater awareness among the general population of the problems besetting Aboriginal people. But she also points out that change was disappointingly slow, no doubt because whites thought the referendum the end of the matter. They did not want to hear of infant mortality rates, of imprisonments, housing problems and grinding poverty (Bandler, 1989: 161—4; also Sykes, 1986:4). Certainly Black activism in Australia cohered in the sixties. It is, after all, of little consequence for Aborigines to be free to choose their lifestyle and assert their cultural identification if they must remain out of hearing politically, economically and socially, that is, stay subjugated.

In the years since the sixties Aborigines have made social gains and in this context white Australians too have made some progress—theirs in terms of understanding something of the problem. But while there have been some improvements in the relationships of Blacks to the dominant white society, and in the attitudes of whites, the enormity and complexity of the challenge can, if anything, be seen even more clearly. Redress for the injustice will be neither swift nor simple, but it must escalate and must be sensitive to fundamental problems. We have already noted that to date, no matter how much Aboriginal people seem to gain, the social differentials between Black and white Australians remain, for as Sykes argues, not only is there an historical basis for the oppression of Aboriginal people, it has a 'contemporary manner of maintenance' (1989:18).

Given the way Aborigines are incorporated into white Australian society, their class relations and how they have been denied social autonomy—even any voice in determining the conditions of their existence—given the history of Black/white relations, in short what it means to be Aboriginal in white Australia, a whole range of affirmative action measures is needed to correct present injustices. The inequalities of opportunities for and in employment must be addressed, but without improving the chances for Aboriginal people across the spectrum of disadvantage, little real and enduring change will be made.

Of recent times our gaze has been directed to the shocking story of Black deaths in custody. A very basic question is why are so many Aborigines caught up in 'the bleak treadmill of arrests and imprisonment' (Reser, 1989:43), for 'Aborigines are more than ten times as likely to be imprisoned and more than twenty times as likely to be placed in police custody than their non-Aboriginal conterparts' (Reser, 1989:43). Sykes observes that Blacks do not see the legal system as protecting their interests, rather they see it as part of their oppression (1989:118). Assuredly they are over-visible in it and overwhelmingly for petty offences. They are, as Sykes writes, excessively policed (1989:139). But further, just as the problems of Aboriginal health, housing, education and employment cannot be understood and should not be addressed in isolation from each other, and even outside the processes of history, so must Black deaths in custody be located in a broader and dynamic social, cultural and historical frame of understanding. That Aborigines were dispossessed of their land and denied much of their culture in their own country was an ugly start to race relations in Australia. That white society has continued in these and other ways to colonise Aboriginal people has maintained distance, mistrust and ill-will as well as underwriting social injustice. And so long as whites (no matter how well-intentioned) make decisions for and on behalf of Aboriginal people and the patronage and control continues, relations will remain fundamentally flawed. There is indeed, a growing recognition that Aboriginal voices must be heard and heeded in negotiating their future.

For migrants

The history of Australia since 1788 is a history of migration. Claimed as British, the colony reflected the values of British society and endeavoured, insofar as was possible in a penal settlement, to replicate its social structures and relations. The power relations of early settlement, mediated by the state, became building blocks in class formation. They established the conditions for the ascendancy of a pastoral elite, for the later development of a mercantile bourgeoisie and for the creation and re-creation of the working class. But whatever the patterns of social relations established in the late eighteenth and early nineteenth centuries, since the first settlers were Anglo-Celtic, the model of Australian society was defined and celebrated as white and identifiably British. Certainly later immigrants, whatever their nationality, have been required to slot into the structural arrangements determined by that model. It is true that social allegiances to 'home' (as Britain was for so long called even by people born in Australia and who had never left it) have weakened markedly. The White Australia Policy has long fallen into disrepute and Britain is no longer saluted as the centre of the English-speaking world. Yet despite the fact that being white and of British stock is not now stressed in quite such a laudatory way (de Lepervanche, 1980:24) there is no doubt that life was and is easier for immigrants of such origins. Individuals from other cultural backgrounds, and less frequently of other colours, have achieved success in Australia but as a general principle, the more distant immigrant groups are from the white and Anglo-Celtic model of society in terms of colour, language and culture, the more they are socially disadvantaged.

Today our rhetoric abjures earlier racist attitudes and celebrates multiculturalism in Australian society. Nonetheless our everyday social relations with recent and even established immigrants are permeated with assumptions of assimilation. We may derive satisfaction from colourful cultural accretions but at the same time as we acclaim the value of cultural diversity we expect immigrants to conform to the traditional social arrangements, behaviours and values, in effect, to the 'Australian way'. As Kalowski points out, the gulf between the rhetoric of multiculturalism and actual behaviour is as great as ever. So much is superficial acknowledgment and treatment, often enough dangerously masking the real issues (1986:10). The truth is that divisions remain and certain structural patterns have developed around the fact of difference. Jakubowicz, Morrissey and Palser query why ethnicity acts as such an important designator of social difference in Australia (1984:iii). The corollary to that question is, why should such social differences work as the building block for social disadvantage? Why is it that migrants, and some especially, are so hobbled in the opportunity stakes?

The establishment and expansion of capitalism in Australia created heavy and urgent, although sometimes uneven, demands for labour. The need for adequate labour reserves has been the prime reason for the large scale of immigration to this country (see Collins, 1984:5). Many of the problems confronting migrants in Australia can really only be well understood in the context of this information. Jakubowicz, Morrissey and Palser argue that the role of the state with regard to immigration policies and migration programs is to uphold the existing social order. In capitalist countries a segmented labour market is integral to that order. The segmentation of the labour market is, at first glance, premised on issues of education and training, occupation and levels of skills. Such factors are, however, in themselves tied to class and recreate class differences. Immigrant workers, particularly migrants drawn from specific regions, have been recruited to the secondary division in the labour force (Collins, 1975). They have been recruited to low paid, low status jobs with poor working conditions. But the people joining the workforce at the lower end of the employment scale are not only immigrants from a working class background. Labour market conditions at any given time are critical in determining whether migrants can find work at all—even work which is not commensurate with their qualifications, their skills and their previous experience. People emigrate for a variety of reasons and over the years many who have come to Australia have not had their qualifications recognised. Some have been required to acquire additional certification and have done so, although this inevitably entails costs in time and in opportunities for achievement. Others have sought employment where they could, sometimes in unrelated occupations and at lower levels. Not all migrants are or become members of the working class but immigration programs, which have been crucial to the development of capitalism in Australia, have provided a large and, given the power structure, generally biddable workforce. The programs have served not only to build up labour reserves on a broad front, but have also responded, from time to time, to the needs of particular markets. Again it is important to stress that migrants have been heavily employed in the lowest paid, least interesting and frequently dirtiest work. Often enough it has also been dangerous work. The point is that for many migrants the disadvantaging processes they experience as migrants are strongly embedded in class relationships—in class formation, in the re-creation of class relationships and in class fragmentation. The condition of the labour market at any given time significantly influences immigration policy. Within these parameters, or perhaps in accordance with them, immigration programs, because they are determined by the state, will subscribe to dominant ideologies. This is so because, as Collins writes, 'the state bureaucracy organises and underwrites the immigration program, determines target intakes and administers policies for migrants on arrival' (1984:3).

Factors of class contributed significantly to the continuing ideological triumph of Albion. Lampugnani and Mansell make the point that between 1901 and 1940 approximately 626 800 migrants entered Australia. They were all British and were essentially from working class backgrounds. They were followed by relatively small numbers of Italians and Greeks who were seen as the answer to demands for cheap labour. Ever since that time, these authors argue, non-Anglo-Celtic migrants have filled low status, low paid occupational positions. The pattern had actually been heralded in the nineteenth century (see, for example, Evans, Saunders and Cronin, 1975). Of recent times there has been a further development relating specifically to non-anglophone migrant women. Alcorso writes that lacking marketable skills and experiencing financial pressures these women provide a source of cheap flexible labour for Australian manufacturing industries. The conditions of their work, their job security, their prospects and their pay are all very poor. In seeking employment, structural and attitudinal racism and sexism afford them little choice (Alcorso, 1989:11).

There are, however, many problems with which migrants struggle which arise outside the frame of class relationships, although they may well contribute to the form of those relationships and be structured by them. For a start, the reasons leading to emigration from the country of origin or even simply of residence may well be fraught with tensions and the decision to emigrate charged with difficulties. Then the very process of migration is dislocating. This is so whatever the status of the individual, whether refugee, independent or dependent, skilled worker, business person or professional. Separation, detachment from networks of family and friends and from a familiar environment, is an early step in that process.

Subsequently there are the pressures of adjusting to a new environment, not only a possibly changed physical environment, which cannot be dismissed as a factor, but a social context in which values, aspirations and expectations are likely to be different and social practices will certainly be so. Any or perhaps all of these difficulties will be exacerbated for non-anglophones. There will also be cross-cutting, thereby compounding problems relating to issues such as education, housing or health. Moreover, there are specific problems facing women, children and aged people, difficult enough on their own account and often most searingly etched in class relations. According to Bradshaw (1984:18−20), migrant women rank 'being isolated from others', often locked in a miserable and crushing existence, as one of the most acute problems. The list is tellingly extended by others to include problems of mental health, industrial health, limited work opportunities, exploitation in employment, cross-cultural conflicts for children, difficulties in adapting family life to Australian circumstances and a sense of ineffectualness in their family role (National Women's Advisory Council, 1979; Devetzidis, 1985). Many of these problems are attributable to language barriers and class credibility although, echoing Alcorso (1989), the actual conditions for their emergence are well-grounded in attitudinal and structural racism.

Kalantzis and Cope (1984) argue that 'migrantness' and poor 'intercultural communication' have an overburden of class. Being ethnically different provides a front for exploitation and oppression. Even when attitudes become more accepting 'the structures and relations of class and gender are still there' and ethnic difference continues to provide, albeit more weakly, a rationale for discrimination. The nub of this analysis is that the difficulties which beset so many migrants in their relations to Australian society are presented as cultural. Two important consequences, really obverse sides of the same construction, result. Migrants themselves, on the basis of their ethnicity, are cast as 'the problem' (Morrissey, 1984) rather than the problems being identified as lying in the immigration program or the systems and structures of Australian society. Thus, not only are migrants made culturally culpable for the difficulties they experience in their new country, but attention is directed away from consideration of evaluation of problems arising from their location in the labour market. Morrissey argues that what we are looking at is 'migrantness as ideology':

> Effectively it locates the origin of the working-class migrant's predicament to a large extent outside the area in which collective social action in Australia might change anything, and certainly it offers no hint that the migrant's *class* relations within Australian society might have anything to do with this predicament. (1984:75)

It is questionable how far EEO programs as we know them can go in addressing the processes which socially disadvantage migrants and in assisting their incorporation, not only into the labour force but if they so choose into the mainstream of Australian society. But while EEO programs are not able, nor do they seek, to get to the root of the problems they can tackle many issues of discrimination in some employment at least (the widespread problems of outwork do not lie in that reach). We must, however, be vigilant in ensuring that programs which recruit migrants to the workforce do not trap them into certain class positions. That is, we must be careful that through EEO we do not endorse and reinforce some biases in class cleavages and in so doing further underline ethnic differences as well as actually limit opportunities for many migrants. There is a story told, and we cannot vouch for its veracity, that a 'strategy' in one EEO management plan produced over recent years was to recruit more migrant women to the part-time cleaning staff of the organisation concerned. If apocryphal the story is cautionary, if it is true it is appalling in its implications. Perhaps what we should be focusing on is not the issue of ethnicity or migrant status, nor even ethnic groups, but as Collins argues, 'classes within each ethnic category, taking into account the migrants, class background and culture, region, religion and time of arrival in Australia' (1984:9).

For people with physical disabilities

In 1977 the Royal Commission on Human Relationships reported that although it is possible to overcome many of the social consequences of physical handicap, the evidence from Australia reveals the inadequacy of responses to these difficulties (1977, Vol 5:114). Physical disability establishes a difference, not simply from the majority but quite overtly from the ideal. In this context there is no question of any rhetoric celebrating difference. But, as ever, the fact of difference generates contradictory reactions. One women interviewed set out the problem most tellingly:

> Society has a double standard about my difference. If I created my difference by dying my hair or shaving it, society would view that as me expressing my individuality, but since my difference has been imposed upon me as a child, that difference is viewed as a reason to segregate me. The problem is not my difference, I am not allowed to be different. (Druett in Lawrence, 1989:33)

Thus difference, already hard to handle when it flies in the face of dominant models of the proper and desirable becomes, when it is imposed not chosen, not only dissonant but implacably refractory. Of course, individuals would prefer not to have a disability, but this must be distinguished from the imperative of sameness in which difference not only provokes discomfort in responses but often enough constitutes a threat. It is from this perspective that the common prejudices devaluing people with disabilities can be most transparently understood.

There is a tendency to adopt a unitary characterisation of people with disabilities which is premised simple-mindedly on the fact of disability, whatever it may be. This is made possible by the force invested in imposed difference. Yet in the first instance it can mask very significant dissimilarities. According to the Royal Commission on

Human Relationships the grouping 'handicapped' is artificial since it may well be that there is nothing held in common except this label (1977:14). For a start individuals are disabled in a range of ways and in markedly varying degrees. Some physical disabilities can be coped with more readily than others which severely limit a person's activities. Even so, while some features are not in themselves inherently limiting they may nonetheless lead to discrimination. (The New South Wales Anti-Discrimination Board cites the example of facial disfigurement; 1979:3.) The totalising effect of an initial classification of disabled, while generally establishing the ground for discrimination, accommodates a variety of responses. They may have little to do with the restrictions attendant on the disability itself, rather on the way it is perceived. Certainly people with an obvious difference are more likely to experience discrimination than those whose problems are less visible although in themselves more limiting. As the New South Wales Anti-Discrimination Board observes: 'Social labelling confers different meanings on different kinds of handicap and in itself this suggests that the limitations confronting indivduals result not only from the physical disability but from widely held social attitudes' (1979:5).

There is also the consideration of whether a person is born with a physical disability or is visited with it later in life. The consequences for the experiences of knowing the world around, of education, of employment, of sexual and social relationships are all likely to differ on this ground.

While it is true that 'genetics is no respecter of persons' and illness or accident can bring disability to anyone, there is some social patterning in the information of disabilities acquired in later life as a result of accident or occupational disease. Certain industrial workers, notably men in mining, transport and rural occupations, and in trades, process and labouring jobs, are clearly at higher risk (see for example, Harrison, Frommer, Ruck and Blyth, 1989). The recent epidemic of repetition strain injury (Hopkins, 1989) while also class-biased, had its greatest impact on women — process workers, piece workers and keyboard operators being particularly vulnerable.

If, Australia-wide, we could eliminate workplace accidents alone (that is not including occupational diseases) for those aged between 25 and 64, we could reduce the disability rate for that group by 46.7 per cent. If there were no workplace accidents there would be 67 500 fewer Australians with physical disabilities (ABS, 1984:31). Disability resulting from occupational disease bumps up those figures although patchy record keeping does not allow direct comparisons. We do, however, know that in the period 1984–85 occupational diseases accounted for 66 deaths in New South Wales alone (ABS:1986). Clearly our work practices contribute significantly to injury and disease leading to disability. Not only is there a class bias in this process but, heeding Collins' argument (1975), it has special consequences for migrants coming originally from some geographical regions.

As we have noted, troubles for people with disabilities do not stop at their physical condition, which in itself can be problematical enough. The dynamic of disability and widely held social attitudes and arrangements renders the disadvantaging process more complex. It becomes cumulative disadvantage in social process and in perception. There is, for example, a common enough expectation that one form of disability is associated with or must lead to another. This mindless extension is potently expressed in the comment: 'People think that because I haven't got one *facility* I haven't got all my *faculties*.' (Dark quoted in Lawrence, 1989:27)

One of the outcomes of physical disability is the likelihood of increasing dependence on others, a dependence which may range from minimal to total. Again, there are problems with the flow-on effects since people in an obvious state of dependence may be thoughtlessly diminished in perceptions of their social worth. More than this, not only are people with disabilities 'objectified, fragmented and commodified' (Nothdurft, 1987:30) but their concomitant marginalisation as social beings has significant consequences for self-esteem; it destroys self-confidence and can generate shame (see respondents' comments in Lawrence, 1989:74, 119). Moreover, dependence and devaluation in this and other contexts gives rise to patronage wherein the positive aspects of support can become clouded by an assertive arrogance. As Nothdurft writes: 'It is offensive to people with disabilities to behave as if the able bodied know what is best for us' (1988:30). Patronage can have the effect of maintaining the relative powerlessness of the client group and participation without power is indeed not only frustrating, it is a meaningless and invidious exercise.

The New South Wales Anti-Discrimination Board sets out various attitudes adopted towards people with disabilities. They include fear and dread, pity, reverence, ridicule, paternalism and embarrassment. Even antagonism can be displayed (1979:27, 136, 178). Is there a fear of contagion, or a sense of 'there but for the grace of God...'? In all events there is a distancing action in all these responses and the attendant isolation, whether imposed or sometimes sought, compounds existing problems of negative attitudes, bias in social relations and discriminatory social structures in a manner which, at the same time, reconstitutes them.

Problems of social participation resulting from physical disability are not confined to any specific areas but the Board nominates four areas which emerge as being important sites of discrimination against people with disabilities. They are: access, education, employment and accommodation. None can be understood by itself. It is, after all, obvious enough how employment options foreclose if education is inadequate. And for various reasons related to their disability but which are structurally embedded, individuals may be strangers to the educational system, receiving an inadequate or inappropriate education in its length, quality and type. It is no more difficult to see how employment may bear on accommodation or even back on education, or how matters of access interact across the range of possibilities. The account, in effect, becomes something of a roundelay.

Throughout any review or analysis of the problems confronting people with disabilities there run a few constant themes, and they too interplay and draw from each other. As we have seen, the devaluing construction of difference and its crudely stigmatising application underwrites most other consideration. It certainly infects a spread of attitudes about worth, ability, potential and rights. On its own account and through other attitudes it prefigures various forms of social closure, in education, in employment, in realms of policy making and in everyday social relationships.

There is another pervasive consideration which has a very material expression — the economic disadvantage which so often results from disability. As the New South Wales Anti-Discrimination Board points out, relative poverty is a normal state of affairs for 'many, if not most people with handicaps'. Exclusion from the paid workforce, and for those in employment from work that is well-paid, the frugality of welfare benefits, medical and associated requirements and the costs of transport all contribute to that economic disadvantage. Even the financial wellbeing of a family may suffer since women in these households are less likely to seek paid employment (Royal Commission on Human Relationships, 1977, Vol 5:117). Nor is it easy to plan for a measure of financial security in more difficult times. The evidence is that insurance of most kinds (life, accident, sickness or motor car) is more difficult for a person with a disability to arrange. The injustice here is compounded by the likelihood of greater need of such insurance. The already demanding and acknowledged challenge for society to review its attitudes to people with physical disabilities, and hence to change its social structures, must be reinforced by the estimates that 'by the year 2000, 50% of the world's population will be suffering from some sort of handicap'. (See New South Wales Anti-Discrimination Board, 1979:6)

Some words to end

Alerted by Pateman's comments (1988:233−4), we note that these words are to end this discussion but they terminate neither the enquiry nor the debate. We hope they may stimulate it. It seems that a root problem in disadvantaging processes lies in the delineation and pronouncement of difference. But this is not in itself explanation of structured social disadvantage. Difference after all is a relative state and the questions arise: different from what? defined by whom and in what terms? In the context of systemic disadvantage it is apparent that difference is not a matter of choice—it is a physical or social characteristic acquired beyond the control of individuals, whether or not they see it as desirable.

Prevailing dominant forms and orders are construed as not only the norm but the ideal. The ideal is premised on the values and interests of the dominant group who have the power to define the normative. Difference from it represents inadequacy, a shortfall in meeting the ideal. It creates groups of 'other', it encapsulates notions of social assymetry, and it prefigures unequal power relationships. Thus difference can be devalued which, given the way benefits are controlled by those with the power, leads directly to disadvantage. It provides a basis for social rejection and social closure. What must be stressed is that endeavours to legitimate social inequalities on the basis of naturalness in either biological or cultural terms are, to put it nicely, misconceived, or less generously, wilfully misleading. Social inequalities are not natural; they are socially constituted and institutionalised and they are maintained through social process. Attempts to reduce inequalities must take account of the disadvantaging processes. Difference, and the political uses to which that is put, provides a pivotal point in the processes of disadvantage. The processes are not, however, the same for each group because of the various ways in which their differences are socially constructed and developed. It is difficult to legislate for social change, even though such legislation really reflects changes already well underway. EEO and other legislative reforms carry their own limitations, inhering in part in their specificity of focus, in the shallowness of their immediate impact and sometimes in their implementation. Yet the alternative to EEO is not to turn away from the quest, not to resile from action—a likely enough reaction to criticism. The useful response is to review the exercise with the intention of making it more appropriate, to use EEO in order, as Harding writes, to 'reveal the nature of the beast through its forms of resistance to "reasonable" demands' (1981:247).

Bibliography

Abramson, J. (1975) *The Invisible Woman: Discrimination in the Academic Profession* San Francisco: Jossey Bass
—— (1979) *Old Boys New Women* New York: Praeger
Affirmative Action Agency (1988) *Annual Report 1987–88* Canberra: Australian Government Publishing Service
—— (1989) *Annual Report 1988–89* Canberra: Australian Government Publishing Service
Alcorso, C. (1989) *Newly Arrived Immigrant Women in the Workforce* A Report for the Office of Multicultural Affairs, Centre for Multicultural Studies, University of Wollongong
Aller, J. (1989) 'Mainstream or Downstream? The Future of EEO in the New South Wales Public Sector' *Refractory Girl* 31–32, pp. 24–30
Australian Bureau of Statistics (1986) *Employment Injuries New South Wales 1982–83 to 1984–85* Catalogue No 6311.1 Sydney
—— (1984) *Handicapped Persons Australia, 1981* ABS Catalogue No 43430. Canberra
Baldock, C.V. (1983) 'Public Policies and the Paid Work of Women' in C.V. Baldock and B. Cass (eds) *Women, Social Welfare and the State* Sydney: Allen and Unwin
Baldock, C.V. and Cass, B. (eds) (1983) *Women, Social Welfare and the State* Sydney: Allen and Unwin
Bandler, F. (1989) *Turning the Tide* Canberra: Aboriginal Studies Press
Banks, O. (1981) *Faces of Feminism* Oxford: Martin Robertson
Barlow, A. (1984) 'The Relationship between Aboriginal Education and Multicultural Education' in Phillips, D.J. and Houston, J. (eds) (1984) *Australian Multicultural Society* Victoria: Drummond, pp. 103–109
Barwick, D., Beckett, J. and Reay, M. (eds) (1985) *Metaphors of Interpretation: Essays in Honour of W.E.H Stanner* Canberra: Australian National University Press
Bean, C.E.W. (1943) *War Aims of a Plain Australian* Sydney: Angus & Robertson
Benokraitis, N.V. and Feagin, R. (1978) *Affirmative Action and Equal Opportunity: Action, Inaction, Reaction* Boulder, Colorado: Westview Press
Béteille, A. (ed) (1969) *Social Inequality* Harmondsworth: Penguin
Biskup, P. (1982) 'Aboriginal History' in Osborne, G. and Mandle, W.F. (eds) (1982) *New History: Studying Australia Today* Sydney: Allen and Unwin, pp. 11–31
Bocher, R.B. (1982) 'Does Tradition Affect Affirmative Action Results? How Pennsylvania Achieved Changes at the Middle Management Level' *Public Administration Review* 42, 5, pp. 475–478
Bonacich, E. (1987) 'The Limited Social Philosophy of Affirmative Action' *The Insurgent Sociologist* 14, 1, pp. 99–116

Bradshaw, D. (1984) 'Since Coming Here...' *Migration Action* VII, 1, pp. 16—21

Brenner, J.A. (1987) 'Feminist Political Discourses: Radical versus Liberal Approaches to the Feminization of Poverty and Comparable Worth' *Gender and Society* 1, 4, pp. 447—465

Brewer, E.C. (1983) [1870] *The Dictionary of Phrase and Fable* London: Cassell

Broom, D.H. (ed) (1984) *Unfinished Business: Social Justice for Women in Australia* Sydney: Allen and Unwin

Bryner, G. (1981) 'Congress, Courts and Agencies: Equal Employment and the Limits of Policy Implementation' *Political Science Quarterly* 96, 3, pp. 411—430

Bryson, L. (1983) 'Women as Welfare Recipients: Women, Poverty and the State' in Baldock, C.V. and Cass, B.(eds) (1983) *Women, Social Welfare and the State* Sydney: Allen and Unwin

Burney, L. (1986) 'Something is Very Wrong' *Education* 67, 4, p. 10

Burton, C. (1984) 'Documenting the Power Structure in Academic Institutions' in Eyland, A. and Buschtedt, I. (eds) (1984) *Equal Opportunity in Tertiary Institutions* Sydney: Macquarie University

—— (1985) *Subordination* Sydney: Allen and Unwin

Carsaniga, G. (1986) 'Varieties of National Identity' *Arena* 74, pp. 39—47

Cass, B. (1983) 'Redistribution to Children and to Mothers: A History of Child Endowment and Family Allowances' in Baldock, C.V. and Cass, B. (eds) (1983) *Women, Social Welfare and the State* Sydney: Allen and Unwin

Cavalier, A. and Slaughter, S. (1982) 'Autonomy versus Affirmative Action: What Price Social Justice?' *Higher Education* VII, 4, pp. 381—395

Chapman, B.J. and Miller, P.W. (1986) 'Immigrants in the Australian Labour Market' *Current Affairs Bulletin* 63, 4, pp. 4—11

Chertos, C.H. (1984) 'Hard Truths for Strategic Change: Dilemmas of Implementing Affirmative Action' in Dudovitz, R. *Women in Academe* London: Pergamon Press, pp. 231—241

Chisholm, S., Knox, H., Wolfe, L.R., Brown, C.G. and Jolly, M.K. (1979) 'An Interview on Title IX' *Harvard Educational Review* 49, 4, pp. 504—526

Church, G.J. 'Every Man for Himself' *Time Magazine* 7 September 1981, pp. 22—23

Clynch, E.J. and Gaudin, C.A. (1982) 'Sex in the Shipyards: An Assessment of Affirmative Action Policy' *Public Administration Review* 42, 2, pp. 114—121

Cockburn, C. (1983) *Brothers: Male Dominance and Technological Change* London: Pluto Press

Cohen, M., Nagel, T. and Scanlon, T. (eds) (1977) *Equality and Preferential Treatment* New Jersey: Princeton University Press

Collins, C. (1989) 'ESSO's EEO Programme—A Case Study.' Paper to Women, Management and Industrial Relations Conference. Macquarie University, Sydney

Collins, J. (1975) 'The Political Economy of Post-War Immigration' in Wheelwright, E.L. and Buckley, K. (eds) (1975) *Essays in the Political Economy of Australian Capitalism* 1, Sydney: Australia and New Zealand Book Co

—— (1984) 'Immigration and Class: The Australian Experience' in Bottomley, G. and de Lepervanche, M. (eds) (1984) *Ethnicity, Class and Gender in Australia* Sydney: Allen and Unwin, pp. 1–27

Commercial Clearing House (1983) *1984 Guidebook to Fair Employment Practices* Chicago: Commercial Clearing House

Connolly, W.E. (1972) 'On "Interests" in Politics' *Politics and Society* 2, 4, pp. 459–477

Cornford, F.M. (1949) [1908] *Microcosmographia Academica, being a guide for the young academic politician* Cambridge: Bowes and Bowes

Cooper, S. (1986) 'Women's History Goes to Trial: EEOC and Sears, Roebuck & Co.—Introduction to the Documents' *Signs* 11, 4, pp. 751–779

Crisp, L.F. (1978) *Australian National Government* Melbourne: Longman Cheshire

Dahrendorf, R. (1969) 'On the Origin of Inequality among Men' in Béteille, A. (ed) (1969) *Social Inequality* Harmondsworth: Penguin.

Davidoff, L. (1976) 'Landscape with Figures: Home and Community in English Society' in Mitchell, J. and Oakley, A. (eds) *The Rights and Wrongs of Women* Harmondsworth: Penguin

Davies, B. (1982) 'Discrimination, Affirmative Action and Women Academics: A Case Study of the University of New England' *Vestes* 25, 2, pp. 15–22

Deal, T.E. and Kennedy, A.A. (1982) *Corporate Culture, The Rites and Rituals of Corporate Life* Reading, Massachusetts: Addison Wesley

Department of Aboriginal Affairs (1984) *Aboriginal Social Indicators 1984* Canberra: Australian Government Publishing Service

Department of Prime Minister and Cabinet (1984) *Affirmative Action for Women. Policy Discussion Paper* Canberra: Australian Government Publishing Service.

—— (1985) *Affirmative Action for Women—A Progress Report on the Pilot Program. July 1984 to March 1985.* Canberra: Australian Government Publishing Service

—— (1985) *Working Party on Affirmative Action Legislation—Report* Canberra: Australian Government Publishing Service

Devetzidis, A. (1985) 'Immigrant Women: Some Comments on Factors Contributing to Health Problems in Immigrant Women *Australian Federation of University Women Bulletin* 24, pp. 26–27

Diprete, T.A. and Soule, W.T. (1986) 'The Organization of Career Lines: Equal Employment Opportunity and Status Advancement in a Federal Bureaucracy' *American Sociological Review.* 51, 3, pp. 295–309

Edwards, M. (1984) 'The Distribution of Income within Households' in Broom, D.H.(ed) *Unfinished Business* Sydney: Allen and Unwin

Eisenstein, H. (1985) 'Affirmative Action at Work in New South Wales' in M.Sawer (ed) (1985) *Program for Change* Sydney: Allen and Unwin, pp. 72–83

Evans, R., Saunders, K.and Cronin, K. (1975) *Exclusion, Exploitation and Extermination: Race Relations in Colonial Queensland* Sydney: Australia and New Zealand Book Co.

Exum, W.H. (1983) 'Climbing the Crystal Stair: Values, Affirmative Action, and Minority Faculty' *Social Problems* 30, 4, pp. 383–399

Ferguson, D. (1985) 'Harassment—Employers Responsible' *Journal of the New South Wales Teachers Federation* 66, 13, p. 9

Ferguson, K.E. (1984) *The Feminist Case against Bureaucracy* Philadelphia: Temple University Press

Fishkin, J.S. (1983) *Justice, Equal Opportunity and the Family* New Haven: Yale University Press

Franzway, S. (1986) 'With Problems of Their Own: Femocrats and the Welfare State' *Australian Feminist Studies* 3, pp. 45—57

Franzway, S., Court, D. and Connell, R.W. (1989) *Staking a Claim—Feminism, Bureaucracy and the State* Sydney: Allen and Unwin

Game, A. (1984) 'Affirmative Action: Liberal Rationality or Challenge to Patriarchy?' *Legal Service Bulletin* 9, 6, pp. 253—257

Game, A. and Pringle, R. (1983) *Gender at Work* Sydney: Allen and Unwin

Gittell, M. (1975) 'The Illusion of Affirmative Action' *Change* 7, 8, pp. 39—43

Goldman, A.H. (1979) *Justice and Reverse Discrimination* New Jersey: Princeton University Press

Gray, A. (1988) *Aboriginal Child Survival* Occasional Paper Australian Bureau of Statistics

Hacker, A. 'Women at Work' *The New York Review of Books* XXXIII, 13, 14 August 1986, pp. 26—32

—— 'American Apartheid' *The New York Review of Books* XXXIV, 19, 2 December 1987, pp. 26—33

Harding, S. (1986) *The Science Question in Feminism* Ithaca: Cornell University Press

Harrison, J.E., Frommer, M.S., Ruck, E.A. and Blyth, F.M. (1989) 'Deaths as a Result of Work-Related Injury in Australia, 1982—1984' *The Medical Journal of Australia* 150, pp. 118—125

Hearn, J. and Parkin, W. (1987) *'Sex' at 'Work'—The Power and Paradox of Organisation Sexuality* Sussex: Wheatsheaf Books

Hiatt, L.R. (1971) 'Secret Pseudo-Procreation Rites Among the Australian Aborigines' in Hiatt, L.R. and Jayawardena, C.(eds) *Anthropology in Oceania* Sydney: Angus and Robertson, pp. 77—88

Hitt, M. and Keats, B.W. (1984) 'Empirical Identification of the Criteria for Effective Affirmative Action Programs' *The Journal of Applied Behavioral Science* 20, 3, pp. 203—222

Hope, D. (1986) 'New law, new threats to get women more "male" jobs' *The Bulletin* 22 April, pp. 58—66

Hopkins, A. (1989) 'Social Construction of Repetition Strain Injury' *Australian and New Zealand Journal of Sociology* 25, 2, pp. 239—259

House of Representatives (Australia) Standing Committee on Legal and Constitutional Affairs (1989) *Submissions on Equal Opportunity and Equal Status for Australian Women* Vols I and II: Canberra

Hughes, E.C. (1944) 'Dilemmas and Contradictions of Status' *American Journal of Sociology* 50, pp. 353—359

Jaffe, A.J. *et al.* (1982) 'Summary Notes on the Statistics of Federal Affirmative Action Programs' *The American Journal of Economics & Sociology* 41, 4, pp. 321—332

Jakubowicz, A. (1981) 'State and Ethnicity: Multiculturalism as Ideology' *The Australian and New Zealand Journal of Sociology* 17, 3, pp. 4—13

—— (1985) 'Ethnic Affairs Policy in Australia: The Failure of Multiculturalism' in Poole, M.E., de Lacey, P.R. and Ranohawa, B.S.(eds) (1985)

124   *Bibliography*

Australia in Transition — Culture and Life Possibilities Sydney: Harcourt Brace
Jovanovich, pp. 271—278
Jakubowicz, A., Morrissey, M. and Palser, J. (1984) *Ethnicity, Class and Social
Policy in Australia* SWRC Reports and Proceedings No 46. Sydney: Social
Welfare Research Centre, University of New South Wales
Jamieson, S. (1989) 'Industrial Relations: Recent Developments and Chal-
lenges'. Paper to Women, Management and Industrial Relations Con-
ference. Macquarie University, Sydney
Jayawardena, C. (1968) 'Ideology and Conflict in Lower Class Communities'
Comparative Studies in Society and History 10, 4, pp. 413—446
Jewson, N. and Mason, D. (1986a) 'Modes of Discrimination in the Recruit-
ment Process: Formalisation, Fairness and Efficiency' *Sociology* 20, 1,
pp. 43—63
—— (1986b) 'The Theory and Practice of Equal Opportunities Policies:
Liberal and Radical Approaches' *The Sociological Review* 34, pp. 307—334
Joint Sub-Committee on Women in the Service (1984) *Affirmative Action
Program for Women in the Australian Public Service* EEO Bureau of the Public
Service Board, Canberra: Australian Government Publishing Service
Jupp, J. (1986) 'The Politics of Multiculturalism' *The Australian Quarterly* 58,
1, pp. 93—101
Kalantzis, M. and Cope, B. (1984) 'Multiculturalism and Education Policy'
in Bottomley, G. and de Lepervanche, M.(eds) (1984) *Ethnicity, Class and
Gender in Australia* Sydney: Allen and Unwin
Kalantzis, M., Issaris, M. and Cope, B. (1985) 'Culture and Merit'. Paper to
Conference on Defining Merit. Macquarie University, Sydney
Kalowski, J. (1986) 'Women in a Multicultural Society' *Migration Action*
VIII, 1, pp. 10—14
Kanter, R. (1977) *Men and Women of the Corporation* New York: Basic Books
—— (1983) *The Change Masters — Corporate Entrepreneurial Work* Unwin Paper-
backs: London
Kaufman, M. (1971) *The Limits of Organizational Change* Alabama: University
of Alabama Press
Kessler-Harris, A. (1987) 'Equal Employment Opportunity Commission V.
Sears, Roebuck & Company: A Personal Account' *Feminist Review* 25,
pp. 46—69
—— (1988) 'The Just Price, the Free Market, and the Value of Women'
Feminist Studies 14, 2, pp. 235—250
Kingston, B. (1981) 'Women and Equity in Australia' in Troy, P. (ed) (1981)
A Just Society Sydney: Allen and Unwin
Lampugnani, R. and Mansell, B. (1984) 'Ethnic Women in the Australian
Labour Force' *Flinders Journal of History and Politics* 10, pp. 40—52
Lawrence, A. (ed) (1989) *I Always Wanted to be a Tap Dancer: Women with
Disabilities* Sydney: New South Wales Women's Advisory Council
Lawrence, P. (1964) *Road Belong Cargo* Melbourne: Melbourne University
Press
de Lepervanche, M. (1980) 'From Race to Ethnicity' *Australian and New
Zealand Journal of Sociology* 16, 1, pp. 24—37
—— (1989a) 'Women, Nation and the State in Australia' in Yuval-Davis, N.
and Anthias, F. (eds) *Women-Nation-State* London: Macmillan, pp. 36—57

—— (1989b) 'Breeders for Australia: A National Identity for Women?' *Australian Journal of Social Issues* 24, 3, pp. 163–182

Levin, M. (1984) 'Affirmative Action: Discrimination against Men and Their Wives'. Australian Festival of Light Resource Paper. November

Lloyd, G. (1989) 'Women as Other: Sex, Gender and Subjectivity' *Australian Feminist Studies* 10, pp. 13–22

Loveday, P. and Cummings, R. (1989) 'Aboriginal Public Servants and Role Conflict'. Paper to Australasian Political Studies Association Anniversary Conference. University of New South Wales, Sydney

Lukes, S. (1974) *Power: A Radical View* London: Macmillan

Lynch, L. (1984) 'Bureaucratic Feminisms: Bossism and Beige Suits' *Refractory Girl* 27, pp. 38–44

Lynn, J. and Jay, A. (1988) *The Complete Yes Minister* London: BBC Books

—— (1989) *The Complete Yes Prime Minister* London: BBC Books

Mannheim, K. (1940) *Ideology and Utopia: An Introduction to the Sociology of Knowledge* London: Routledge and Kegan Paul

Marx, K. [1843] 'Critique of Hegel's Doctrine of the State' in Colletti, L. (ed) (1975) *Karl Marx Early Writings* Harmondsworth: Penguin

Mathews, L. (1985) *Health and Safety at Work* Sydney: Pluto Press

McGuiness, P.P. 'Why "Positive Policy" Harmful' *Financial Review* 29 September 1988

Merton, R.K. [1940] 'Bureaucratic Structure and Personality' in Merton, R.K. *et al.* (1952) *Reader in Bureaucracy* New York: Free Press, pp. 361–371

Michels, R. [1915] *Political Parties* 1962 edn. New York: Free Press

Milkman, R. (1986) 'Women's History and the Sears Case' *Feminist Studies* 12, 2, pp. 375–400

Milward, H. and Swanson, C. (1979) 'Organizational Response to Environmental Pressures — The Policy of Affirmative Action' *Administration & Society* 11, 2, pp. 123–143

Mistilis, N. (1985) 'Second Generation Australians: Progress and Puzzles' *The Australian Quarterly* 57, 4, pp. 288–299

Moir, H. (1984) 'Comment on Women in the Australian Labour Force' in Broom, D.H. (ed) (1984) *Unfinished Business: Social Justice for Women in Australia* Sydney: Allen and Unwin

Moore, W.E. (1962) *The Conduct of Corporations* New York: Random House

Morrissey, M. (1984) 'Migrantness, Culture and Ideology' in Bottomley, G. and de Lepervanche, M. (eds) (1984) *Ethnicity, Class and Gender in Australia* Sydney: Allen and Unwin

Morton, F.L. (1984) 'The Supreme Court's Promotion of Sexual Equality: A Case Study of Institutional Capacity' *Polity* XVI,3, pp. 467–483

Nagel, T. (1977) 'Equal Treatment and Compensatory Discrimination' in Cohen, M., Nagel, T. and Scanlon, T. (eds) (1977) *Equality and Preferential Treatment* New Jersey: Princeton University Press

National Occupational Health and Safety Commission (1987) *Safe Manual Handling* Discussion Paper and Draft Code of Practice. Canberra: Australian Government Publishing Service

New South Wales Anti-Discrimination Board (1979) *Discrimination and Physical Handicap* Vols I and II Sydney: New South Wales Goverment Printer

—— (1983) *Annual Report* Sydney: New South Wales Government Printer

Nothdurft, J. (1987) 'You Too Could Have a Body Like Mine—Discrimination and Disability' in New South Wales Anti-Discrimination Board *Making Rights Work* Sydney: New South Wales Government Printer, pp. 23—31

Nothdurft, J. and Astor, H. (1986) 'Laughing in the Dark—AntiDiscrimination Law and Physical Disability in New South Wales' *The Journal of Industrial Relations* 28, 3, pp. 336—352

OECD Working Party (1984) Report on the Role of Women in the Economy. *Occupational Segregation by Sex* MAS/WP6 (83)5 Paris: Organisation for Economic Cooperation and Development

O'Donnell, C. and Hall, P. (1988) *Getting Equal* Sydney: Allen and Unwin

Office of the Director of Equal Opportunity in Public Employment (1982) *Annual Report* Sydney: New South Wales Government Printer

—— (1983) *Annual Report* Sydney: New South Wales Government Printer

—— (1984) *Annual Report* Sydney: New South Wales Government Printer

—— (1985) *Annual Report* Sydney: New South Wales Government Printer

—— (1986) *Annual Report* Sydney: New South Wales Government Printer

—— (1989) *Annual Report* Sydney: New South Wales Government Printer

—— (n.d.) *Equal Employment Opportunity Management Plan Resurvey 1985 Preliminary Report* Sydney: New South Wales Government Printer

Over, R. (1981) 'Women Academics in Australian Universities' *Australian Journal of Education* 25, 2, pp. 166—176

Partington, G. (1984) 'Women in Australian Universities' *Quadrant* 197, pp. 127—129

Pateman, C. (1981) 'The Concept of Equity' in Troy, P.(ed) (1981) *A Just Society* Sydney: Allen and Unwin

—— (1985) 'Women and Democratic Citizenship' The Jefferson Memorial Lecture delivered at The University of California, Berkeley, February

—— (1988) *The Sexual Contract* Cambridge: Polity Press

—— (1989) *The Disorder of Women* Cambridge: Polity Press

Pear, R. 'Study Says Affirmative Rule Expands Hiring of Minorities' *New York Times* 19 June 1983

Phillips, A. (1987) *Divided Loyalties: Dilemmas of Sex and Class* London: Virago

Piper, D.W. and Glatter, R. (1977) *The Changing University—A Report of the Staff Development in Universities Program 1972/74* Windsor: NFER Publishing Company Limited

Poiner, G. (1990) *The Good Old Rule: Gender and Other Power Relationships in a Rural Community* Melbourne: Sydney University Press in association with Oxford University Press

Power, M. (1975) 'Women's Work is Never Done by Men: A Socio-Economic Model of Sex Typing in Occupations' *Journal of Industrial Relations* 17, pp. 225—239

Price, Waterhouse, Urwick (1989) 'Industry Perspectives on Issues Surrounding Affirmative Action Legislation' Melbourne

Public Service Board (1984) *Affirmative Action Programs for Women in the Australian Public Service* Canberra: Australian Government Publishing Service

—— (1986) *Annual Report 1985—86* Canberra: Australian Government Publishing Service

Public Service Commissioner (1989) *Annual Report 1988—89* Canberra: Australian Government Publishing Service

Radford, G. (1985) 'Equal Employment Opportunity Programs in the Australian Public Service' in M.Sawer (1985) *Program for Change* Sydney: Allen and Unwin, pp. 51—71

Rawls, J. (1971) *A Theory of Justice* Cambridge, Massachusetts: Harvard University Press

Reich, M., Gordon, D.M. and Edwards, R.C. (1980) 'A Theory of Labor Market Segmentation' in Amsden, A.H. (ed) (1980) *The Economics of Women and Work* Harmondsworth: Penguin

Reser, J. (1989) 'Aboriginal Deaths in Custody and Social Construction: A Response to the View that there is no Such Thing as Aboriginal Suicide' *Australian Aboriginal Studies* 2, pp. 43—50

Reskin, B.F. (1988) 'Bringing the Men Back In: Sex Differentiation and the Devaluation of Women's Work' *Gender & Society* 2, 1, pp. 58—81

Reynolds, H. (1981) *The Other Side of the Frontier* Townsville: James Cook University of North Queensland

Rhode, D.L. (1986) 'Feminist Perspectives on Legal Ideology' in Mitchell, J. and Oakley, A. (eds) (1986) *What is Feminism?* London: Blackwell, pp. 151—160

Riger, S. (1988) 'Comment on Women's History Goes to Trial: EEO *v.* Sears, Roebuck & Company' *Signs* 13, 4, pp. 897—903

Robinson, D. A. (1979) 'Two Movements in Pursuit of Equal Employment Opportunity' *Signs* 4, 3, pp. 413—433

Roe, J. (1983) 'The End is Where we Start From: Women and Welfare since 1901' in Baldock, C.V. and Cass, B. (eds) (1983) *Women, Social Welfare and the State* Sydney: Allen and Unwin

Ronalds, C. (1987a) *Australian Report for OECD Working Party on the Role of Women in the Economy Monitoring Panel on Equal Employment Opportunity Programs and Policies* Department of Prime Minister and Cabinet, Canberra

—— (1987b) *Affirmative Action and Sex Discrimination* Sydney: Pluto Press

Rothschild, E. 'The Reagan Economic Legacy' *The New York Review of Books* XXV, 12, 21 July 1988, pp. 33—41

Rowley, C.D. (1972a) *The Destruction of Aboriginal Society* Ringwood: Penguin

—— (1972b) *Outcasts in White Australia* Ringwood: Penguin

—— (1972c) *The Remote Aborigines* Ringwood: Penguin

Royal Commission on Human Relationships (1977) *Final Report* Vol 5, Canberra: Australian Government Publishing Service

Sawer, M. (1984) *Towards Equal Opportunity: Women and Employment in the Australian National University* Canberra: Australian National University

—— (1987) 'Two Steps Backwards: Equal Opportunity Policy under Howard and Hawke' *Politics* 22, 2, pp. 92—96

Seitz, A. and Foster, M.L. (1985) 'Dilemmas of Immigrations—Australian Expectations, Migrant Responses: Germans in Melbourne' *The Australian and New Zealand Journal of Sociology* 21,3, pp. 414—430

Selznick, P. [1949] 'Cooptation: A Mechanism for Organizational Stability' in Merton, R.K. *et al* (eds) (1952) *Reader in Bureaucracy* New York: Free Press, pp. 135—139

Sher, G. (1977) 'Justifying Reverse Discrimination in Employment' in Cohen, M., Nagel, T. and Scanlon, T. (eds) (1977) *Equality and Preferential Treatment* New Jersey: Princeton University Press

Slater, R. (1986) 'Negative Reaction to Affirmative Action' *Quadrant* XXX, 1 & 2 (219), January—February, pp. 44—45

Sloan, J. and Kriegler, R. (1984) 'Technological Change and Migrant Employment' *The Australian Quarterly* 56, 3, pp. 216—226

Smith, L.R. (1980) *The Aboriginal Population of Australia* Canberra: Australian National University Press

Smith, R.F.I. and Weller, P.(eds) (1978) *Public Service Inquiries in Australia* St. Lucia: University of Queensland Press

Sokoloff, N.J. (1988) 'Evaluating Gains and Losses by Black and White Women and Men in the Professions, 1960—1980' *Social Problems* 35, 1, pp. 36—53

Spender, D. (1982) *Women of Ideas and What Men Have Done to Them* Routledge and Kegan Paul: London

Staines, G., Travis, C. and Jayartne, T.E. (1974) 'The Queen Bee Syndrome' *Psychology Today* 8, January, pp. 55—60

Stanner, W.E.H. (1968) *After the Dreaming* The Boyer Lectures Sydney: Australian Broadcasting Commission

Steinberg, R. (1987) 'Radical Challenges in a Liberal World: The Mixed Success of Comparable Worth' *Gender and Society* 1, 4, pp. 466—475

Stevens, F. (1974) *Aborigines in the Northern Territory Cattle Industry* Canberra: Australian National University Press

Stewart, J. and Bullock, C. (1981) 'Implementing Equal Education Opportunity Policy—A Comparison of the Outcomes of HEW and Justice Department Efforts' *Administration & Society.* 12, 4, pp. 427—446

Strombach, T. (1986) 'Immigration as a Source of Skills' *The Australian Quarterly* 58, 2, pp. 183—191

Summers, A. (1975) *Damned Whores and God's Police* Ringwood: Penguin

Sykes, R. (1986) *Incentive, Achievement and Community* Sydney: Sydney University Press

—— (1989) *Black Majority* Melbourne: Hudson

Thompson, E. (1986) 'Reform in the Public Service: Egalitarianism to the SES' *Politics* 21, 2 pp. 41—50

Thornton, M. (1983) 'Job Segregation, Industrialisation and the Non-Discrimination Principle' *The Journal of Industrial Relations* 25, 1, pp. 38—50

—— (1984) 'Changing University and College Acts of Incorporation' in Eyland, A. and Buschtedt, I. (eds) *Equal Opportunity in Tertiary Institutions* Sydney: Macquarie University Press

Villiers, A.D. (1986) 'Legislating for Women's Rights and Conservative Rhetoric—Lessons for Feminists'. Winner of 1986 Australian Institute of Political Sciences Women and Politics Prize

Walby, S. (1986) *Patriarchy at Work: Patriarchal and Capitalist Relations in Employment* Cambridge: Polity Press

Waring, M. (1988) *Counting for Nothing—What Men Value and What Wonen are Worth* Wellington: Allen and Unwin and Port Nicholson Press

Weber, M. [1947] (1966) *The Theory of Social and Economic Organization* New York: Free Press

Wertheim, B. (1985) Report to Public Service Board of New South Wales on Management Fellowship Study

Wilenski, P. (1977) *Directions for Change: Review of New South Wales Government Administration — Interim Report* Sydney: New South Wales Government Printer

—— (1982) *Unfinished Agenda: Review of New South Wales Government Administration: Further Report* Sydney: New South Wales Government Printer

—— (1985) 'Equal Employment Opportunity — Widening the Agenda' *Canberra Bulletin of Public Administration* XII, 1 pp. 42–46

Wills, S. (1983) 'Perceptions of Discrimination: Realism — Not Paranoia' in Cass, B., Dawson, M., Temple, D., Wills, S. and Winkler, A. *Why So Few? Women Academics in Australian Universities* Sydney: University of Sydney Press

Wright, L. (1989) 'Women Carry the Burden of Our Fears' *The Sydney Morning Herald* 17 July

Yeatman, A. (1990) *Bureaucrats, Technocrats, Femocrats — Essays on the Contemporary Australian State* Sydney: Allen and Unwin

Young, R.M. (1979) 'Why Are Figures So Significant? The Role and the Critique of Quantification' in Irvine, I. and Evans, J. *Demystifying Social Statistics* London: Pluto Press, pp. 63–76

Ziller, A. (1980) *Affirmative Action Handbook* Sydney: New South Wales Government Printer

Zinn, M.B. (1989) 'Family, Race and Poverty in the Eighties' *Signs* 14, 4, pp. 856–874

Index

130